ISBN 978-1-331-38777-0
PIBN 10183161

This book is a reproduction of an important historical work. Forgotten Books uses
state-of-the-art technology to digitally reconstruct the work, preserving the original format
whilst repairing imperfections present in the aged copy. In rare cases, an imperfection in
the original, such as a blemish or missing page, may be replicated in our edition. We do,
however, repair the vast majority of imperfections successfully; any imperfections that
remain are intentionally left to preserve the state of such historical works.

The Curriculum of the Horace Mann Elementary School

By

The Teachers of the Horace Mann Elementary School

Teachers College, Columbia University

Reprinted from the March and May, 1913, Teachers College Record
Second Impression, October, 1914

35570

PUBLISHED BY
Teachers College, Columbia University
NEW YORK CITY
1913

CONTENTS

TEACHERS OF THE HORACE MANN ELEMENTARY SCHOOL

1912-1913

Henry Carr Pearson	*Principal*
Clara Mabel Wheeler	*First Grade*
Florence Mabel McVey	*First Grade*
Evelyn Batchelder	*Second Grade*
Mildred Ione Batchelder	*Second Grade*
Alice Elizabeth Phelps	*Open Air Class*
Mary A. Oliver	*Open Air Class*
Myrtle Garrison	*Open Air Class*
Roxana A. Steele	*Third Grade*
Alice Thompson	*Third Grade*
Ida Elizabeth Robbins	*Fourth Grade*
Florence May Marshall	*Fourth Grade*
Elizabeth Cleasby	*Primary Grades*
Maud Vivian Keyes	*Fifth Grade*
Margaret Condry	*Fifth Grade*
Lura Parker Fitch	*Fifth Grade*
Mary Frederika Kirchwey	*Sixth Grade*
Mary Gertrude Peabody	*Sixth Grade*
Siegried Hansen Upton	*Sixth Grade*
Caroline Woodbridge Hotchkiss	*Seventh Grade*
Lillian Emily Rogers	*Seventh Grade*
Georgia Farrand Bacon	*Seventh Grade*
Kate Stuart Anthony	*Domestic Art*
Lucia Williams Dement	*Fine Arts*
Helen Latham	*Music*
Amy Logan	*Domestic Science*
Robert Josselyn Leonard	*Industrial Arts*
Lucy Hess Weiser	*Industrial Arts*
Marie Karcher Brooks	*French*
Laura Bishop Crandon	*German*
Mary Perle Anderson	*Nature Study*
Florence Mary Healy	*Physical Training*
Marie Louise Dowd	*Physical Training*
P. Joseph Kersey	*Physical Training*
Florence Stuart	*Physical Training*
Fay Williams	*Physical Training*
George Thomas Holm	*Swimming*
Gertrude T. Harris	*Grammar Assistant*
Gertrude Bigelow	*Primary Assistant*

CURRICULUM OF HORACE MANN ELEMENTARY SCHOOL

INTRODUCTION

Henry Carr Pearson

The curriculum of the Horace Mann Elementary School, as published in five numbers of the TEACHERS COLLEGE RECORD in 1906 and 1907, has long since been out of date as well as out of print. In response to many requests, therefore, this revision of the course of study is published.

The changes from the former curriculum, while they are numerous, have been the result of a gradual growth during the past six years. The administration of the school leaves the principal and the teachers peculiarly free to modify their methods of teaching and the subject matter of instruction whenever it seems best to do so in view of the best interests of the pupils and in accordance with the best accepted educational practice. The specific changes that have been made are noted in the introductory statements under each subject.

The Study of New York City, which is outlined in Chapter IV, is an organized attempt to prepare our pupils to take a more intelligent and enthusiastic interest in civic betterment. As they become better acquainted with local history and tradition and with our best artistic possessions, as they come to realize the great social problems growing out of the industrial life of their city and the organizations of good citizens that are working to solve such problems, we hope that they themselves will soon develop a high type of civic responsibility.

There will be noted an attempt in some subjects to organize the subject matter around certain large, fundamental questions or problems. In actual school-room procedure this method is used more than is apparent in this published curriculum. We have found that this method of approach to lessons stimulates interest in the pupils, gives a pointedness to the instruction, and furnishes situations that are favorable to good thinking. As we shall have more experience with this type of teaching, we expect to learn ways and means of carrying it still further and of organizing our curriculum more and more upon this basis. An ideal curriculum may be conceived to be a group of problems of vital interest to children and dealing with the fundamental aspects of knowledge, but at present we are able only to approximate such an ideal.

This statement of the curriculum is organized from the standpoint of the conventional school subjects, rather than from the point of view of the grade, as was the case in the curriculum of 1906. This may give the impression that these school subjects are sharply differentiated from one another. Such is not the case, however, as this curriculum works itself out in the life of the child, for there is much natural correlation and interaction between the different subjects. At the same time we try to avoid the disadvantages of making correlation an end in itself, and of thereby denying the child the opportunity of feeling the logical unity of each subject.

It has been our purpose to have this curriculum reflect the experience and opinion of the entire teaching staff of the school. As a result the outlines were first prepared by various committees of teachers and then presented to the whole group for discussion and modification. After subsequent conferences with the principal and supervisors the outlines assumed their present form.

ARITHMETIC

The general tendency in the teaching of elementary mathematies at the present time seems to point first, toward the introduction of problems which have to do with the conditions of life in the sections where the pupils live; second, toward a kind of drill which shall make for greater speed and accuracy in the four fundamental processes; third, toward enlisting a broad-minded and self-dependent attitude in the pupil's approach to problems; and fourth, toward a familiarity with numbers through their daily use in manual arts and games. That thoroughness in mathematics can never be gained by pupils except through interest has been plain for more than a century. So the old mechanical routine drill has gradually been transformed until in the modern schools we find a new and wideawake activity which extends and amplifies in the class room those experiences of the family and social life which have to do with numbers.

In the elementary grades teachers have been studying to provide a number background related at all points with everyday life. That arithmetic has a place, and an important one, in such everyday life for the average citizen, we are convinced. That the habits of accuracy and concentration upon one's work which this study inculcates are as much as ever necessary, we have daily proof. In a letter to a leading newspaper of New York City, a prominent merchant of wide experience recently commented on the increasing inaccuracy of our young people. In the growing carelessness and inattention to details, which all classes of employers have to contend with in their workers, lie strong arguments for renewed attention to the study which makes for carefulness and for close attention to and correctness of detail. In the need so apparent at the present time of better home and business economics, we see the necessity of so relating our arithmetic to daily life that every citizen may be prepared to cope skillfully with his own economic problems.

There are several main lines along which the normal activities of social living have to do with number. From very early times man has loved the rhythmic repetition of forms, colors, sounds, and motions. He has kept scores or a tally in some fashion. He has loved to barter. Children still love to do these very things, and can be led to an acquaintance with mathematics along these lines with ease, interest, and profit. There is not the slightest reason why learning about numbers should not be as pleasurable and spontaneous as learning to read, and it should begin, too, at about the same period of the child's life. Arithmetic gives him, moreover, the opportunity of overcoming obstacles, which, rightly presented, is a source of greatest joy. There is a keen intellectual delight in solving difficult problems which the older generation knew, and which should not be denied to the younger.

The subjoined course of study in arithmetic was planned by a committee of teachers especially interested in mathematics, and was discussed and revised by the entire teaching force of the school working together in a series of meetings. We have tried in it to bring the subject up-to-date by weeding out those topics no longer in use in the life of to-day, and by introducing others of current interest. We have taken into account the children's natural love of repetition, of playing games with numbers, and of keeping score. We have insisted upon thorough reviews at the beginning of each year. The course as here planned calls for seven years of arithmetic. We hope, however, by greater concentration all along the line, and by pushing forward some of the business arithmetic into the Sixth Grade, to complete most of the work in six years. This will leave the seventh year free to take up elementary work in algebra and geometry.

In the First Grade work, number games with large domino cards and with a modified shuffle board and with other devices, combined with counting and measuring, supply the larger part of the number study. The pupils choose sides in the games and the leader keeps score on the blackboard, thus easily and naturally learning to write figures. The leaders change from day to day so that all may have opportunity for practice in the scorekeeping. The greater part of the exercises in industrial arts involves measuring, as does also the garden work, so that the children gain thereby considerable facility in dealing with numbers. There is no text-book work, but every opportunity to introduce numbers in distributing material, counting material, and other class-room activities, is utilized by the teacher.

In the Second Grade more formal work begins. The pupils count as indicated in the outline and are drilled to do so accurately and rapidly. Often they judge of time by counting, clapping hands, hopping or skipping in time to the count, thus bringing into play the rhythmic repetition beloved by primitive races. Oral and written addition and subtraction drills are given, and written work not involving carrying is placed on the blackboard. From counting, the pupils learn the multiplication tables through ten times five, while the inverse cases of these introduce them to division. With objects they find halves and fourths of numbers, and through much practice in measuring lengths and liquids learn to handle these two fractions readily. In this way they also learn the relation of pint to quart, of quart to gallon; of inch to foot, and of foot to yard. As the pupils write combinations on the blackboard, the signs of addition, subtraction, multiplication, and division, are supplied by the teacher when the need arises, until through use they grow familiar. Telling time by the clock becomes vitally interesting this year and furnishes an opportunity for teaching the Roman numerals I to XII. The number games before school and at odd moments call now for higher scores and for more difficult operations, and, with the work in industrial arts, call for and give closer familiarity with numbers and measures. Near the close of the year the pupils are given a text-book.

Each year commences with a thorough review of the previous year's work, but we try to have the reviews from year to year vary sufficiently to seem new to the pupils. With a summer vacation of four months, these reviews are not only important but indispensable, especially in the earlier grades where the fundamental number combinations are taught.

After reviewing the Second Grade work, the Third Grade teacher has much to accomplish. The multiplication tables are completed through twelves with rhythmic motion drills and other devices similar to those of the preceding year. The pupils play store and bring various articles to school which are sold for toy money. This game, which is of absorbing interest, introduces a great variety of number operations. The pupils invent many little problems in connection with this game, make change, become more familiar with the various coins, and get much drill of an interesting sort in addition, subtraction, multiplication, and division. The written subtraction of the grade involves numbers of four orders; in addition, where numbers of three orders only are added, the sum does not exceed four orders; in multiplication and division, the multipliers and divisors respectively are of one order, the multiplicands and dividends of four orders. The effort is always to work with numbers which will seem real to the children and to keep close to the concrete. Thirds, sixths, and eighths are the new fractions this year and much use of them is made in measuring.

The Fourth Grade work is so closely associated with that of the Third Grade that thorough review is especially important. The counting is continued and, besides that involved in the multiplication tables, variety is introduced by beginning with 1, 2, etc., to 10, and adding 2's, 3's, etc., to 12's. The pupils are taught to use freely the terms sum, addend, minuend, subtrahend, difference, multiplier, multiplicand, product, dividend, divisor, and quotient, in speaking of the numbers used in the various processes. Long division is the principal feature of the year's work. In preparation for it the pupils are drilled in reading and writing numbers to one million. After the process of long division has been thoroughly made clear, the emphasis of the work is upon drill for speed and accuracy, and the text-book gives a variety of examples designed for this use. Care has to be taken lest, in their zeal for learning the new process, pupils forsake short division entirely, and we are compelled to insist strongly that short division be used wherever divisors are of one figure, or of one figure followed by ciphers. In this grade, too, the common weights and measures are formally set forth in tables and memorized. Problems from the text-book involving but one process are explained and solved by the pupils.

The counting contests in Grade Five, where children choose sides and count by sixes, sevens, eights, and nines, serve as a review and a rapid drill. The work of the year is the gathering up of the facts about fractions already learned in the lower grades, and the application of the four fundamental processes of addition, subtraction, multiplication, and division to work with the common and decimal fractions used in daily life. A card game in addition and subtraction is used at odd minutes. The pupils make and solve simple problems, in addition to those supplied by the text-book, involving the use of common and decimal fractions. Problems from the household milk bills, which in our city are always made out in eighths, fourths, or halves of pints and quarts, prove interesting and very practical. The industrial arts lessons also call for much use of small fractions.

Counting in Grade Six is amplified by using 25, 33⅓, 8⅓, 15, and 16 as the units in addition to those already used in lower grades, thus paving the way for the use of business per cents to come. A thorough drill in percentage is the main feature of this grade, applying it constantly to the uses of daily life. Thus the pupils find the average of mistakes in their own papers, the percentage of answers correct, the number of pupils absent each day, and what per cent are present, etc. In their games and in scoring there are other opportunities of finding the percentage of games won per side, the percentage lost, etc., until the percentage idea becomes a familiar and practical one. The text-book gives many practical problems along the same lines, but some of our best problems are made by the pupils themselves. For those in discount, they frequently use the lists of mark-down sales found in circulars sent to their houses by the big department stores or taken from the advertisements in the daily papers. For those in interest, they use their own savings bank books. In their geography text-book they find data which help them to reckon the percentage of foreign-born citizens of each nation, and in connection with nature-study they reckon the air pressure in storms.

In the Seventh Grade a general review of arithmetic, with special emphasis on the principles underlying each process, is undertaken. The pupils are shown the importance in this review of thoroughly understanding the fundamental processes of arithmetic, so that they may be better equipped for the business of life. As the fundamental work of the year is to be " business operations," the pupils are zealous to understand and apply the facts of numbers and to acquire facility in handling numbers. As in all the grades the custom is to devote the first five minutes of each recitation to some form of rapid drill varied from day to day to meet the needs which arise. Every third week addition records are kept, each pupil striving to outdo himself in five minutes' intensive addition by keeping his own score from day to day. After a week the scores are put away, and counting to review the multiplication tables takes the place of the addition, then rapid fire drill in division and subtraction are substituted for another week. After a few weeks the pupils return to their addition, refreshed and prepared to make yet higher scores.

The work in business operations is introduced by lessons in keeping accounts, in the uses and kinds of banks, and some preliminary instruction is given in writing orders for goods and in making out bills, drafts, and notes. Then comes the practical application. Each pupil selects a business, and is given a sum of money in school currency. The room is thrown open for trading and the pupils make out written orders, bills, to be paid by check, draft or money order. All papers are subject to the teacher's approval. Mistakes of any sort are subject to fines in school currency, the teacher and pupils checking each other. A bank of deposit is opened in which all money is deposited to be drawn upon for the payment of accounts, and each pupil balances his own ledger daily. The time given to this work is one period a week for about twelve weeks. Meanwhile, at other periods, the pupils discuss and solve the text-book problems in ratio and simple proportion, in mensuration, in longitude and time, and in the use of the simple equation. The business periods serve as a strong incentive to proficiency in the other work, as only pupils who are efficient in this are allowed to compete for the position of cashier in the school bank. The cashiers serve for one month only and take entire charge of the bank ledger and bank books which are checked up at the end of the month, errors being subject to fine.

FIRST GRADE

Counting. Let the pupils count from 1 to 100 by 1's, from 10 to 100 by 10's. Drill often enough to gain rapidity in counting.

Addition. Teach concretely all combinations of two numbers whose sum does not exceed ten.

SUBTRACTION. Teach the inverse cases of addition. Work for speed and facility in both addition and subtraction through handling a variety of material.

MEASURES. Teach the children to recognize and compare the inch and foot; the cent, nickel, dime, and dollar; the day, week, month, and year.

SYMBOLS. Teach the figures 1, 2, 3, 4, 5, 6, 7, 8, 9, and o.

PROBLEMS. Give many oral problems connected with industrial arts and gardening, and involving only one operation.

RECREATIONS. Let the pupils play dominoes and other games involving simple additions and subtractions or counting.

SECOND GRADE

Review work of Grade I.

COUNTING. Have the children count by 2's to 20, beginning with o and 1; by 3's to 30, beginning with o, 1 and 2; by 4's to 40, beginning with o, 1, 2 and 3; by 5's to 50, beginning with o, 1, 2, 3 and 4, in preparation for addition and multiplication tables.

ADDITION. Teach the children to add, o, 1, 2, 3, 4, 5, 6, 7, 8 and 9, to any number not exceeding ten. Oral work should predominate, this being followed by written work evolved from it. In the written work no " carrying " should be involved.

SUBTRACTION. Let the inverse cases of addition be taught as in Grade I.

MULTIPLICATION. Teach the tables through 10 times 5.

DIVISION. Teach the inverse cases of the above tables and give exercises in finding halves and fourths of numbers.

In all four operations work for facility in handling numbers rapidly and accurately.

FRACTIONS. Teach the children to add and subtract halves and fourths by using the measures taught in Grade I.

SYMBOLS. Use the signs of addition, subtraction, multiplication, and division as may seem advisable, putting little stress upon them. Teach the writing of numbers to 1,000; teach the Roman numerals of the clock face, I to XII.

MEASURES. Teach the quarter and half dollar; foot and yard;

pint, quart, and gallon; how to tell time by the clock; and how to write the current date.

PROBLEMS. Give problems as suggested in the preceding grade and involving the new relations learned this year. Give also problems in measuring the looms and boxes made in industrial arts lessons.

RECREATIONS. Continue more difficult domino and other number games.

TEXT-BOOK. Smith's "Primary Arithmetic" may be introduced this year or postponed to Grade III at the discretion of the teacher.

THIRD GRADE

Review thoroughly the work of Grade II.

COUNTING. See Multiplication.

ADDITION. Review the 45 combinations with applications. Give much rapid oral drill on single column addition.

Teach written addition with numbers of three orders including dollar and cents, involving "carrying."

SUBTRACTION. Teach the making of change. Give frequent rapid oral drill, handling material when necessary as in Grade II.

Teach written work with numbers of four orders in which some of the digits of the subtrahend exceed those of the minuend.

MULTIPLICATION. Continue counting through 12's, thus completing the tables. Let oral work predominate.

Written: Teach the multiplication of numbers of four orders by numbers of one order.

DIVISION. Give much oral drill within the multiplication tables.

Written: Teach the division of numbers of four orders by numbers of one order.

FRACTIONS. Halves, thirds, fourths, sixths, eighths. Oral work in addition, subtraction and reduction.

MEASURES. Teach and compare the ounce and pound; the square inch and square foot. Use these measures in illustrating the multiplication tables.

SYMBOLS. Reading and writing of numbers as required. Roman numerals to XX.

PROBLEMS. Let the pupils make and solve original problems of one step and also solve simple problems from text-book.

TEXT-BOOK. Smith's " Primary Arithmetic " to page 129.
RECREATIONS. Playing store and number games.

FOURTH GRADE

Review systematically the work of the preceding years.

COUNTING. Drill on counting by 2's, 3's, 4's, etc., to 12's, beginning with 1, etc., to 10 and keeping within the limits of the multiplication tables.

ADDITION AND SUBTRACTION. Continue making change as in Grade III. Give much rapid oral work, using tens and units, laying special stress on combinations where nine occurs. Give written work with numbers of four or more orders, checking all answers. Use familiarly the terms sum, addend, minuend, subtrahend, difference.

MULTIPLICATION AND DIVISION. Introduce multipliers and divisors of two and three orders. Always, where divisors are less than 13 and where divisors are multiples of ten, encourage the use of short division. Use constantly the terms multiplier, multiplicand, product, dividend, divisor, quotient, remainder.

FRACTIONS. Continue work of the Third Grade.

MEASURES. Use these as in Grade III and change from lower to higher denominations. Set forth the common weights and measures in the form of tables.

SYMBOLS. Teach the children to read and write numbers to one million. Roman numerals XX to L.

PROBLEMS. Smith's " Primary Arithmetic," pages 129-222. Analyze the problems and give approximate results. Solve the entire problem where this seems advisable.

RECREATIONS. Playing fire-engine game, keeping game score in various ways. Use other number games whenever there seems any advantage in so doing.

FIFTH GRADE

Review thoroughly the work of Grade IV.

COUNTING. Continue as in Grade IV, with much drill on 6's, 7's, 8's and 9's. Add, counting by 12½ and by 16⅔ to 100, also by 20 to 200.

COMMON AND DECIMAL FRACTIONS. Teach the four operations, using only the small fractions of ordinary business. Give concrete work continually and apply the subject particularly to industrial arts.

Let oral work precede and dominate the written work. Teach factoring and use constantly in addition to terms previously mentioned, the words plus, minus, factor, multiple, mixed number, proper and improper fraction, numerator, and denominator. Reduce common fractions to decimal fractions, and vice versa.

PROBLEMS. Solve simple problems involving the use of small common and decimal fractions, and make out simple bills and accounts. Check the problems constantly. Teach the casting out of nines as a check on multiplication.

SYMBOLS. Roman numerals to 100.

Measures: Use the fractional part of the foot, yard, rod; pound, ounce; pint, quart, gallon; peck, bushel.

RECREATIONS. Counting contests.

SIXTH GRADE

Review common and decimal fractions.

COUNTING. Teach, in addition to previous work, counting by 25 to 200, $33\frac{1}{3}$ to 100, $8\frac{1}{3}$ to 100, 15 to 90, 16 to 48 and review the work in counting done in all the lower grades.

DENOMINATE NUMBERS. Teach the reduction of common denominate numbers and give a brief drill in the four operations, using numbers of but two denominations with practical applications to the grade lessons in sewing and carpentry.

PERCENTAGE. Drill upon common business per cents and their fractional and decimal equivalents, changing from one form to another until these are well fixed in the memory. Teach the different cases in percentage by using them in practical problems. Use constantly the terms plus, minus, reduce, reduction, lower and higher terms, sum, difference, amount, per cent of, rate, percentage, product, quotient, and all the common arithmetical terminology.

Teach simple interest, discount, commission, profit and loss.

PROBLEMS. Teach formal analysis of problems in steps and continue the judging of probable results. Employ various methods of checking results, and always insist on some check being used.

In written problems have the analysis written side by side with the work, its importance insisted upon, and the steps numbered.

TEXT-BOOK. Smith's " Grammar School Arithmetic," pages 90-213, omitting mensuration and the more difficult problems for analysis.

SYMBOLS. Roman numerals to M.

RECREATIONS. Team work and contests in counting and in rapid drills.

SEVENTH GRADE

REVIEW. Give a general review of arithmetic, with special emphasis on mechanical efficiency and with some attention to the principles underlying the processes already learned. Give a little of the history of these processes.

RATIO. Teach ratio as a form of comparison by division and apply it in solving problems. Teach simple proportion as an equation and apply it in measuring heights.

BUSINESS OPERATIONS. Teach how to keep and balance simple accounts and how to make out and use such business papers as bills, drafts, orders, checks and notes. Show how to compute interest by 6% method.

LONGITUDE AND TIME. Relate this to the work being done in geography, dwelling chiefly upon the subject of Standard Time.

MENSURATION. Teach the children to find the area and dimensions of the rectangle, triangle, circle, and trapezoid. Use paper cutting for the development of this work. Apply the table of cubic measure in finding the contents of boxes, etc.

PROBLEMS. Continue the work of Grade VI and teach the solutions of text-book and original problems by the use of the simple equation.

TEXT-BOOK. Smith's " Grammar School Arithmetic," pages 214-234, 254, 311, 326-346, 369-390.

RECREATIONS. School banking and business transactions. Card games in multiplication and division, in constructive geometry. Arithmetical puzzles.

GEOGRAPHY

INTRODUCTION

The earth is the home of man. He lives upon its surface, moves over its waters, and breathes the air which envelops it. It prompts and influences his energies. Through his efforts to adapt himself to the physical laws and conditions which govern the earth, man learns to understand the laws, to respect the conditions, and to adjust the earth's resources, so far as possible, to meet his needs. Therefore, a study of the earth without considering the life and work of mankind would be dry and meaningless and would make our work ungeographical.

This point of view has guided our work in the past and still controls it, in spite of the many changes recently made in the course of study. The character of these changes, outlined below, is twofold. First, we have tried to select from the mass of geographic details which fill our modern text-books, those which seem to bear most directly upon the economic and social life of the peoples of the globe, and from the body of facts still further to determine an " essential minimum " which every grammar school pupil should possess. Secondly, the order and presentation of this minimum have been arranged with the aim of making sure that it becomes a " permanent possession."

The reasons for beginning geography with observations in the home field are too well known to need defending here. Our children come to school along crowded thoroughfares; below the ground, above it, and on its surface, they see the movement of peoples and commodities. The city is the child's laboratory, and it is to this busy life that we must appeal for notions with which he may image the remote areas beyond his vision. Home geography and history, therefore, are begun in the Third Grade through a study of the early history of Manhattan Island. The idea of trade and exchange is the basis for our study of the Indian life on the island and the later civilization of the Dutch

14

and English, this in turn leading to the use of the globe and finally to a brief consideration of the belts of extreme temperature and the people who inhabit them.

No exhaustive study of home environment and conditions can be made in primary grades, but by the time our pupils leave the elementary school they should possess a distinct geographic knowledge of their city and state; moreover, we have failed if we have not developed in them some ability to image and interpret things beyond their horizon by means of things seen and handled. Realizing that this power of imagination and interpretation grows with maturity, we have made a place for home geography in every year where geography is a part of the curriculum, placing the emphasis in each year on the aspects of the subject best fitted to the pupil's experience and interest. This makes possible a fuller realization of our ideal to use continually the old related knowledge to comprehend the new, and makes impossible the practice of closing the door on one continent when another is begun.

In the Fourth Grade the work on the home environment grows out of the ideas gained in the Third Grade, that New York is a great trading center, that there is, therefore, a necessity for rapid means of transportation and communication. A brief study is made of our streets, tunnels, and bridges; how they knit together the scattered parts of our city; how traffic is accommodated and expedited; and how our streets are made safe and attractive for city dwellers. In this year the study of a continent first begins. Certain topics from North America are selected and the work is based upon man's need for food, clothing, and shelter. Where and how the raw products are obtained, manufactured, and distributed, and the influence of climate, soil, and surface upon these products form the chief topics of the year. The pupil observes weather conditions and interprets the distant from the near; he studies the kinds of soil about him and gains a notion of the geographical conditions in the great agricultural areas of the United States and Canada. As he works with textiles and clays in his study of the industrial arts, he learns something of the processes required and the labor necessary to change the raw material into the finished product and to carry it where it is needed. He is drilled, also, in the location of a few important places.

Home geography in the Fifth Grade means a knowledge that New York is the chief gateway for the thousands of foreigners who flock every year to our shores, that for this reason it is a more cosmopolitan city than London, and that of necessity it plays an important part in the government regulation of immigration. From the knowledge of the country's resources gained in the Fourth Grade, our need of the immigrant and his willingness to leave the land of his fathers and seek a new home is explained ; in fact, our school rooms are themselves a laboratory for building up these notions. We believe that such a study will give a realization of the original sources of our growing American nation, and develop a more sympathetic appreciation of the contributions each of the alien people gives to our national and city life. It is through some such approach as this that Europe is studied. Our growing trade relations with South America and the effect of the opening of the Panama Canal upon these relations form a motive for the lessons on South America.

Not much stress can be laid upon causes in the first three years of geography, but in the Sixth and Seventh grades the knowledge which our pupils have gained through observation and experience is made the basis for a discussion on the simpler reactions between man and his environment. By means of simple experiments which bear directly upon questions arising from these discussions many of the physical laws which govern our life on a planet are explained. In teaching Africa and Australia the controlling purpose is to show the activities of the colonizing nations of Europe and how these activities are influencing the primitive peoples with whom they come in contact. During the last half of the year certain topics on North America are selected for study, these topics bearing a very direct relation to the periods of Discovery and Colonization which form the basis of the work in United States history. New York State is the topic in home geography in the Sixth Grade, emphasis being laid on the geographic conditions influencing the development of the state and upon man's responses to this control.

In the Seventh Grade the work on North America begun in the Sixth Grade is continued, and United States and its dependencies are studied in detail. But in view of the underlying principle controlling our course, this is not the study of an isolated continent. The opportunity offered by the recent entrance of the United States into world affairs is seized upon for a general world review, and to this is added a particular study of our Asiatic neighbors on the opposite shores of the Pacific, in this way contrasting the highly organized states of society in these older colonizations with the freer, unconventional conditions of the western continent. Such a study shows that though details of development may be different in different nations, yet the primitive needs of man, after all, form the chief motives for his reaching into the varied domains of industry, science, and art, and for his forming world empires which are rapidly knitting together the peoples of the globe.

That the economic and industrial ideas which form the chief control of this course of study must be simple does not detract from their value. In fact, such a point of view vitalizes and unifies all our school work, for it is evident that geography can and must contribute a large share in building up those industrial concepts which the school must furnish its pupils if they are to meet the demands which present social and economic conditions are forcing upon them.

The reference books and text-books used throughout the grades are:

The Dutch Twins, Fitch.
ˇ A Home Geography of New York City, Straubenmüller.
Carpenter's Readers of the various continents.
Chamberlain's Series, How We are Clothed, Fed, and Sheltered.
Industrial Studies, Allen.
Geography of Commerce and Industry, Rocheleau.
From Trail to Railway, Brigham.
Elementary Commercial Geography, Adams.
Representative Cities of the United States, Hotchkiss.
Dodge's Advanced Geography.
Tarr and McMurry's New Geographies.
Longmans' School Atlas.

THIRD GRADE

   I.   Idea of Trade or Exchange.
  II.   Introduction to a Study of the World.
III.   Study of Local Weather Conditions.

In the Third Grade the aim is to give the children experiences which will form a basis for more definite geography work in the later grades. Little attempt is made to formulate a set body of geographical facts; but rather to arouse an interest in people and things. It is very difficult to separate the geography and history in this grade, and since it may all come in the same period the three parts of this outline are used parallel rather than in sequence.

I. Idea of Trade or Exchange

1. As carried on to-day between pupils and between different localities. These ideas are made clear by two excursions. The children go to 130th Street ferry to see exchange going on there. They note the barges going up and down the river, carrying coal, lumber, bricks, etc. They also go to a large wholesale market where all kinds of food supplies are brought in. In class work the children suggest things in the home which are brought from foreign countries and tell how they are brought here.

2. Trade among the Indians on Manhattan Island itself and between Indians on the island and those across the river. Children suggest the articles that might have been exchanged and the means of exchange.

3. Trade carried on between the Dutch and the Indians as brought about by Hudson's discovery and through Adrian Block. Brief study of the Dutch in their own country finds a place here.

4. New Amsterdam as a trading center. Its advantages of location are noted, its excellent harbor, its water connections with other parts, also the quantities of material found on the island and in the vicinity that the Dutch wanted, such as furs, lumber, etc.

5. The purchase of Manhattan Island by Dutch traders.

6. The establishment of a village around the trading post. Children discuss what would be the buildings necessary in such

a village, the homes, the church, and schoolhouse, the storehouse, the fort. They also consider the industries likely to be carried on, *viz.,* trade in furs and lumber, the beginning of farming and manufacturing, chiefly in the home.

The Dutch in Their Own Country

1. Character of the country: Low and flat with many canals and windmills, the extensive water-front, thus prompting many to a sea-faring life.

2. People. The general appearance, customs, and industries, emphasizing the trading with other countries made easy by access to water. Globe used to show the respective positions of Holland and India and the difficulties of trading partly by water and partly by land.

3. Attempt of Dutch to find a shorter passage to India. Emphasis laid on Henry Hudson's expedition, his motive, the description of his boat, comparing it with the ocean liner of to-day, the helps he had in sailing, charts and compass, the story of the entrance of the " Half Moon " into the harbor of New York, the meeting between the Dutch and the Indians, and the trip up the river. Maps and sand table used to fix locality and to picture the surface of the island in those early days.

4. Results of Hudson's discovery.

II. INTRODUCTION TO A STUDY OF THE WORLD

1. Direction. Children find where sun sets and get other directions from that. They draw a compass on the floor and correct by a real compass. They make a compass with a magnetized needle in dish of water. A drawing of a compass is made and hung with the north always at top. Directions from classroom of familiar places in neighborhood are given. This work is then transferred to paper, bringing out *map* idea.

2. Map drawing to easy scale. Table, desk, room are drawn.

3. Use of globe. Children recall trips they have made, and tell direction in which friends going to Europe have sailed. Steamship lines to Europe are named and direction pointed out, also position of countries to which the ship is going.

4. Land and water masses distinguished. Continents and

oceans are named, giving direction of continents and countries from New York. Small globes are used.

5. Belts of extreme temperatures and their countries. (a) Land of the Eskimo. (b) Land of the Arab (Desert).

III. Study of Local Weather Conditions

Incidental work on wind, temperature, length of day. Sunny and shady sides of streets contrasted, north and south entrances to school, location of garden with reference to sunshine, the drying of sidewalks on windy and calm days, etc.

The following lesson on one of the topics referred to under the " Idea of Trade or Exchange" is suggestive of the method of treatment in this grade.

Study of a Wholesale Market

The keynote of the geography of the Third Grade is the idea of trade or exchange as carried on at home and in the immediate neighborhood, and this serves as an introduction to the study of world relations and interdependence through trade which is carried further in the succeeding grades.

A study of the immediate locality in its community aspect is made, beginning with the home, its members, and their interdependence. The type of home, whether in private house, apartment, or hotel is next considered, and its dependence on the neighboring grocer, butcher, and delicatessen shop. The convenience with which our needs are supplied is emphasized, for we note that through delivery wagons, automobiles, telephones, and messengers our wants are immediately satisfied. This leads to the questions:

1. How do our local dealers get their supplies? Children suggest farms and wholesale markets.

2. What is a wholesale market and where is it located? Teacher and children determine to answer the last question by a visit to such a market.

TRIP MADE TO GANSEVOORT MARKET ON WEST 14TH STREET

Some of the large topics noted and discussed were the following:
1. The variety of foods found there.
2. Packing and storing of these foods.
3. Meaning of commission merchant.
4. Foreign countries represented through labels.
5. Means of transportation and local delivery.

In the discussion that followed the excursion the children decided to make a class record of their experience. Two questions arising from this discussion prompted the following work:

1. Which of the products we saw can be grown at home and which come from a distance?

2. Why can we raise these foods here and not others?

Lists of home products were put on the board with a view to making a collection of pictures of them. From magazines and catalogues children collected and mounted pictures on a chart which was called "Home Products." In discussing the second question statements of climatic and soil conditions were written on the board by the teacher and copied by the children as a class story. In the same way a chart called "Foreign Products" was made, labels from cans and packages being used instead of pictures.

It was decided to make a class book, each child selecting a topic to write upon. A few of the many topics suggested are given below:

Why We Went to the Market.
Why the Market is Situated Where It Is.
Market Time.
Open Space where the Farmers Come.
How Meat is Brought to the Wholesale Market.
Cold Storage and Ice Houses.
Where Some of the Things Come From.
Traffic.

Each child chose his own topic and wrote upon it. The English was corrected by the teacher and children, then the paper was copied and added to the book.

Through the above study the children were impressed with the bigness and importance of their city and of the world at large, and they felt they had a speaking acquaintance with many countries beside their own.

The following are samples of pupils' work that grew out of such an excursion to a market.

LABELS*

All goods at the wholesale market must have labels to prevent the selling of stale goods. The labels tell where the goods come from. Some oranges come from California, and some from Florida. We have a book of labels showing where things are packed. It is interesting to see how far they have traveled to reach New York.

* Individual work.

FOREIGN PRODUCTS*

These fruits and vegetables we cannot grow here so we call them foreign products. Many of these fruits come from the south where it is very warm and rainy and where they have long summers. Some of our best apples come from the western part of our country and from the northern part of our own state which is cold.

Our foreign products are brought to us from all over the world in trains and boats. They are taken to the wholesale markets and the retail grocers buy from them and sell to us.

* Class story.

FOURTH GRADE

   I.   Home Geography Continued.

  II.   The World as a Whole.

III.   North America—Emphasis on the United States.

The introduction of the text-book in this grade necessitates a careful study of its proper use. Consequently the teacher and pupils together spend several class periods in solving from the text-book typical problems of study. This familiarizes the pupils with the proper use of the maps, pictures, text, and reference tables, and at the same time furnishes excellent training in right habits of study.

The means of transportation and communication form the special topic for home geography in this grade. This naturally follows the topic of the preceding grade, and also furnishes an approach to an elementary idea of the world as a whole.

Emphasis in the grade, however, is placed mainly on a study of the United States from the standpoint of its chief industries.

Children are taught to use intelligently such geographical terms as continent, hemisphere, river system, river valley, mountain range, mountain system, plateau, and plain. Throughout the year, in addition to the text-book, frequent use is made of lantern slides, pictures, collections, and the experience of the pupils in the school garden.

In this and in succeeding grades, much emphasis is placed upon visualizing and memorizing the location of the important cities, rivers, lakes, and mountains.

I. HOME GEOGRAPHY

Means of Transportation and Communication

The necessity for roads is shown through the child's experiences and through the knowledge of trade and the exchange of commodities gained in the Third Grade. Our school is situated on a historic thoroughfare, and Amsterdam Avenue is linked with the city's history through its name. Stories of early modes of travel are told to emphasize the present ease, safety, and speed of communication in New York and the effect of this on trade and industry. The city paves, lights, cleans, and repairs the streets, while the child shares the responsibility for their care, appearance, and beauty.

Bridges and tunnels connect our island borough with widely scattered land masses belonging to the city and vicinity. Elevated roads, subways, street railways, steam railways, and water ways are needed to move people and goods quickly to and from the city. The Hudson is a highway of traffic, a moving road. The kinds of bridges children have crossed, the material of which they are made, are noted and pictures collected and compared.

II. THE WORLD AS A WHOLE

From the study of the great city with its rapid means of communication linking it to all countries, the children pass to a consideration of the world as a whole. The shape of the earth is here assumed, a more detailed study of the results of living on a spherical earth being taken up in the Sixth Grade. Imaginary journeys across the seas are taken and the names of continents, islands, and oceans are reviewed and learned. The direction of other countries from New York and from each other is a feature of this study. The work on the Heat Belts of the third year is reviewed and enlarged. The ideas presented are made concrete and vivid by a discussion of life conditions in these climatic belts and by collections of fruits, nuts, grains, spices, etc., which the children bring at Thanksgiving time and arrange on shelves, grouping according to the belts in which they grow. The countries in which these products grow are then found, named, and located.

III. North America—Emphasis on the United States

A knowledge of the United States is obtained by studying the great industries that stand out most strongly in our country, *viz.,* agriculture, grazing and dairying, lumbering, hunting and fishing, manufacturing, and commerce. By suggesting to the pupils certain problems, such as,—Why does cotton grow so abundantly in the South? How is it possible for the United States to send so much wheat to other countries? Why does most of the meat in our New York markets come from the West?—they gain an idea of geographical conditions in certain great sections of our country. In such a study emphasis is placed on the physical conditions that have influenced the habits and customs of the people.

The following are some of the geographical and industrial facts learned through a study of farming in the Central Plain. The detailed study of wheat is given as a type of work along other lines.

Prairies and Great Plains

Extent of region as a whole, including Canada. Boundaries. Red River Valley.

Surface: Generally level. Long gradual slopes drained by rivers. Importance of rivers.

Soil: Productive and non-productive areas.

Climate: Summer and winter temperatures and winds. Amount and distribution of rainfall.

Products: Wheat, corn, cotton, sugar cane, sugar beets, fruits. etc.

Wheat: Appearance of wheat farm, size, buildings necessary. Preparation of ground for planting. Appearance of seed and plant. Harvesting. Life of farmer and his family, comforts, pleasures, etc.

States engaged in wheat raising.

Cities Engaged in the Making of Flour

Shipping of grain and flour and routes by which they are transported.
Location of shipping ports and manufacturing centres: Duluth, Chicago, Buffalo, Minneapolis, St. Louis, Winnipeg, Montreal, Quebec.
Foreign countries dependent on United States and Canada for wheat.

Corn, cotton, and sugar cane are treated in a similar way.

In summarizing the work on the United States, the country is divided into the different sections or groups of states. The essential facts of each group are taught.

Topics deserving emphasis in the New England group are:

Names of states in group.
Location in northeastern United States.
Coast line: Very irregular, numerous bays and islands.
Surface and drainage: Hilly and mountainous. White Mountains, Mt. Washington.
Hills low near coast but land gradually rises toward the interior until it becomes a plateau. Plateau crossed by many rivers—Connecticut, Merrimac, Penobscot. Abundance of waterfalls, rapids, and lakes.
Soil: In valleys good. Hillsides poor and stony. Boulders.
Climate: Severe winters, mild summers. Prevailing wind from west, but changes frequently bringing rain. Winter busy season for cutting timber, logging camp.
Industries, varied: Dairying, lumbering, manufacturing, market gardening, fishing, quarrying.
Products: Raw and manufactured.
Cities: Boston, Providence, Fall River, New Haven.
Transportation routes. Boston a centre.
People.

The various groups of states are treated from the same point of view. The knowledge of Canada and Mexico acquired in this grade is largely incidental and obtained by way of comparison.

FIFTH GRADE

   I. Home Geography continued.
  II. Europe.
 III. South America.

The topic in Home Geography selected for this grade is "Immigration and the Foreign Population of New York City." This topic not only has a peculiar value of its own but also serves as an introduction to the study of Europe, to which the greater part of the year is devoted.

This study of Europe centers around certain typical problems that deserve emphasis in the different countries. Some of these problems are:

1. Why is the United Kingdom the greatest exporter of manufactured goods?

2. Prove that Switzerland is the playground of Europe as well as the workshop of the Swiss.

3. Why is Russia called " The Land of Silence "?

By solving intelligently such questions we hope that the pupils will gain a working knowledge of the physical, industrial, commercial, and descriptive aspects of the different countries. By proposing similar problems for study, a general knowledge of South America is gained.

Locational geography is considered very necessary in this grade. Drill lessons to obtain actual knowledge about a few important places and peoples are frequently given.

I.   Home Geography

The topics for Home Geography in this grade are Immigration and the Foreign Population of New York. The main question presented to the pupils is, " Why should New York have such a large foreign population?" In the answer to this question the following points are made:

Population of the United States in 1790—3,000,000.
Population of the United States in 1912—93,000,000.
Where has a large part of this increase come from?
　From Africa: Negroes equal one-tenth of total population.
　From Europe: northern countries, southern countries.
　From Asia: eastern countries.
What has brought them here? Opportunities for work because of: fertile soil, manufacturing, mining.
Why is New York the great gateway through which they pass into the continent? Because of its nearness to Europe, the centre for great steamship lines, and the ease with which all parts of our continent can be reached from New York.
Why should so many immigrants remain in the city? Opportunities for unskilled labor in making of clothes, making tunnels, repairing streets, building, etc.

What are the nationalities in the city? Italian, German, Scandinavian, Irish, Hungarian, Greek, Russian, etc.

What does each contribute toward our city life?

> Greeks: Florists and fruit venders.
> Italians: Fruit venders, dig our subways, builders.
> Irish: Policemen, contractors, builders.
> **Poles:** Work on street and in factories.
> Russians: Make clothing.
> Germans: Business men, musicians.

What does city do for them?

> 1. Establishes schools, parks, libraries, museums, model tenements.
> 2. Protects and cares for the immigrants at Ellis Island.
> 3. Social work done by individuals and by organizations.

II. EUROPE

The following is a summary of the essential facts of Europe which we hope to bring out by the solution of certain related problems.

Europe—General

Importance in the progress of the world.

Location: Favorable position among the continents; its northern latitude; waters.

Size: Smallest of the continents but one. Comparison with United States. Importance in proportion to size.

Coast features: Extent of coast line. Innumerable bays, fjords, rivermouths, and other arms of sea furnish great opportunities for trade. Comparison with North America.

Surface: Mountain areas, highlands, lowlands. Great extent of productive land.

Drainage: Many wide-mouthed, navigable rivers flowing into seas free from ice. Growth of large cities and distribution of population.

Climate: Prevailing westerlies not obstructed by mountains in Central Europe. Temperature and rainfall.

Life: Plant and animal.

Countries: Great Britain, France, Germany, Italy, Austria-Hungary, The Netherlands, Belgium, Norway, Sweden, Russia, Switzerland.

The method used in studying the various countries of Europe is indicated by the following series of lessons on The Netherlands.

The Netherlands—A Type

Work in home geography affords a growing interest in the Dutch. We locate their country and study them in their home environment.

Before studying the topics outlined below, class interest is obtained by reading selections from "Hans Brinker" and a short description in Carpenter's "Europe," dealing with the industries of the country. The solution of the discovered problem gives a definite purpose for considering physical conditions that are in part responsible for the life and industries of the country.

Problem: "Why is grazing an important industry in The Netherlands?"

Review: Locate grazing regions studied in United States and Canada.
  Recall conditions favorable for grazing:
    1. Surface generally level.
    2. Climate not suitable for agriculture:
      a. Rainfall.
      b. Temperature.
Location: Political map.
  Surrounding countries and waters: Latitude with reference to 40th parallel. Comparison with New York.
Size: Extent. Comparison.
Surface: Physical map in Atlas.
    1. The Rhine Basin. Application of study of general surface map, noting peculiarities of surface.
    2. Dykes: Their purpose, size, care; stories, pictures.
    3. Dunes: Nature's aid in helping to shut out the sea. Influence of sand and prevailing westerlies.
    4. Reclaimed lands. Fitting for use, draining, canals, pumps, windmills.
  Use made of winds.
Grazing: Application of surface conditions favorable for grazing to reclaimed and other sections. Comparison with United States. Among Alps.
Temperature: Atlas.
  July temperature. Comparison with New York and United States. Application of temperature conditions favorable for grazing.
Rainfall: Atlas.
  Influence of prevailing westerlies. Application and comparison with United States.
Summary: Solution of problem.
  Because of the generally level land, range of temperature, and distribution of rainfall, grazing may be carried on in The Netherlands.
Dairying: Result of grazing. Comparison with United States. Alps.
Cattle: Kind. number, care, cleanliness, sheds. Comparison with United States. Alps.
Life of the People: Comparison with cowboy life. Life among the Alps.

Butter and cheese: The making. Centres of dairying. Markets at home and abroad, their location.

Industry of towns depends upon accessibility of raw products, nearness to markets demanding products, ease of transportation.

Transportation: Routes. Ports from which shipped, Rotterdam, Amsterdam.

III. SOUTH AMERICA

Argentine Republic, Chile, Brazil, Bolivia, Panama, and Peru are taught in detail. A comparison is made between the great plain of Argentine with its cattle and sheep ranges, wheat fields, railways, cities, and foreign trade, and the great plain of the United States. Panama, a hot, mountainous, narrow country, virtually under the protection of the United States, receives special attention. An idea of the size, time necessary to dig, the cost, and effect on trade of the world of the interoceanic canal now being built by the United States government, is brought out.

After a series of lessons has been given on a country or continent, the children select facts to be memorized. Both the facts and judgment necessary in their selection are of value to the pupil. A lesson on Typical Seaports of South America is given below as one type of drill work.

Drill Lesson

Principal Seaports of South America.

Period—30 minutes.

Work proceeded very rapidly.

Interest in lesson aroused through an article, published by the New York *Times,* on "Floating Exhibition of American Manufactures to South American Ports" for the purpose of increasing trade.

Certain paragraphs of the article selected and read in class.

List of principal ports to be visited, as given in article, placed on board and named.

Name of country in which each port is located, given and placed opposite name of city.

La Guayra	Venezuela
Para	Brazil
Pernambuco	Brazil
Rio Janeiro	Brazil
Buenos Ayres	Argentine Republic
Montevideo	Uruguay
Valparaiso	Chile
Callao	Peru

1. On political wall map of Western Hemisphere, children trace route of the Exhibit Ship from New York to ports in South America naming places to be visited.

2. Call names of places rapidly, and ask different children to locate cities by pointing on wall map.

3. Children ask each other to point to and name cities on wall map.

4. Call for definite oral location of all cities on the Atlantic; on the Pacific.

5. On physical map children find and locate all cities to be visited.

6. Point to and locate orally the city that is the outlet for the greatest river system of South America.

7. Point to and locate orally the city that most closely resembles San Francisco in its location.

8. Find and locate a city that is the outlet for a valley resembling our Mississippi.

9. Locate city that has the largest harbor.

10. Divide class into two sections for quick competition. Pupils in "A" section give name of country. Pupils in "B" section respond by locating city in country. Pupils leave section when mistake is made.

11. Place a "blackboard" outline map before class. Children volunteer to locate cities from memory, by placing city mark and printing name on map.

12. Class check work by referring to map.

13. Pass individual outline maps of South America. Pupils are given a chance to see how many cities they are able to locate within a given time.

SIXTH GRADE

I.   Geographical Principles.

II. Africa, Australia, Eastern North America.

III. Home Geography—The State of New York.

The first portion of the year is devoted to a study of geographical principles. This work is supplemented by the science study of the grade, which is devoted largely to the elements of physical science and thus often serves to elucidate some of the principles involved in the geographical course.

In approaching the study of a continent or a section, the attention of the class is often centered upon some large question, the solution of which involves a considerable body of geographical knowledge. Such questions or problems are stated at the beginning of the detailed outlines given later.

The facts brought out in the preliminary surveys of Africa and

Australia are rather general in character, and have to do with the larger physical features.

The study of the individual sections or countries is far more detailed in regard to both the physical and the life conditions. This latter phase of geography, emphasizing particularly industrial and commercial activity, is the goal toward which all the work tends; the former phase, the physical, is considered as explanatory of these life conditions. This does not mean, however, that *position, surface, drainage,* and *climate* are studied formally as isolated topics, the information to be applied in some future work. On the contrary, they are given immediate point and meaning by being studied when a knowledge of these physical conditions is found to be an essential step in the solution of some important problem. The outlines below suggest this method of procedure, that on Africa being typical of the work on Australia, and that on the Congo Basin, of the study of individual countries and sections of both Africa and Australia.

Eastern North America is studied in four sections; New England as a manufacturing region, the Middle Atlantic states as a commercial section, the South Atlantic states as an agricultural group, and the St. Lawrence Valley as the highway of Eastern Canada. New England as outlined below is typical of the work done on the other sections.

The home state is studied in more detail than is any other section. Again the physical features are considered in their relation to life conditions. The following regions are studied as intensively as the age of children permits: the Hudson and Mohawk Valleys, the Adirondacks, the Highlands, and the Plateau Section.

I. Geographical Principles

1. Form and Size of Earth:
   Early belief that it was flat. Effect on exploration.
   Proofs that it is round. Shadow of earth when cast upon the moon is always circular. The unbroken horizon line is always circular. Circumnavigation proves curvature, not rotundity.
   Circumference. Diameter.
2. Rotation:
   Gives day and night. Fixes noon. North and south line found at noon by means of a shadow stick. Axis, poles, equator defined.

3. Latitude and Longitude:
    Their use. Practice in finding latitude and longitude on maps.
Exact directions found by following meridians and parallels. Approximate time found at various places—New York, London, Algiers,
Cape Town, Melbourne.
    Standard Time. Time Belts in use in the United States. Changes
made in traveling eastward—in traveling westward.
4. Revolution—Inclined Axis:
    Gives change of seasons. Show by means of diagrams and ap-
paratus that when the northern hemisphere is having summer, the
southern is having winter. Compare Cairo and Cape Town.
    Length of day and night at Equator, at Polar Circles, at Poles.
5. Climate:
    Temperature:
Isothermal maps studied. Land and water temperatures compared,
coast and interior, Equator and poles. Shifting of Heat Equator.
    Winds—Rainfall:
Effect of temperature on circulation of the air. The characteristics
of each wind belt studied—the heavy rains of the Doldrums, the fair
weather of the Trades, the stormy Westerlies, etc.

II. Africa, Australia, Eastern North America

Type of Preliminary Treatment of a Continent

Africa

Why has the development of Africa been much slower than that of
the other great continents?

1. Location:
    Not favorable. Almost wholly in the Hot Belt. Compare with
South America. Find latitude of extreme north, of extreme south.
Compare latitude of Algiers and Cape Town with that of Buenos
Ayres, Los Angeles.
2. Coastline:
    Regular—few good harbors. This has repelled sailors. Compare
with Europe and South America. Name and locate principal indentations.
3. Surface:
    Mountains form a rim about the continent and thus are a barrier
to exploration. Compare a trip up the Congo or Nile with ease
of entrance to North America by way of Mississippi and St. Lawrence, to South America by Amazon, to Europe by Danube.
    Name and locate principal highlands, coastal lowlands.
4. Drainage:
    Some of the greatest rivers of the world, but all interrupted by
falls and rapids. Effect on development of country. Nile, Congo,

Niger, Senegal, Zambezi Orange, Vaal studied, general directions and characteristics noted. Compare in size and importance with Mississippi, Amazon, Danube.

Lakes Chad, Victoria, Tanganyika, Nyassa compared in size and commercial importance with the Great Lakes.

5. Climate:

Temperature: Great heat one of the chief causes of slow development. Isothermal maps.

Rainfall: Much of the continent uninhabitable because of too much or too little rainfall—Jungles, Deserts.

Apply work on Wind Belts. Sahara a Trade-wind desert. Winds from northeast blow from a cooler to a warmer region and so absorb moisture rather than give it. Southeast Trades leave moisture on windward side of mountains—result, the Kalahari Desert.

Jungles—Doldrum Belt—great heat—moisture, swamps—unhealthful.

TYPE OF TREATMENT OF A SECTION

The Congo Basin

Henry M. Stanley explored this region and made it known to the world. His journey from Lake Tanganyika down the Congo to the sea, with the difficulties and dangers he encountered, is the basis of the work on this section.

1. Location of river, where it rises, general direction, where it empties, number and size of its tributaries.

   Compare length of Stanley's trip with a trip down the Mississippi, down the Amazon.

2. Character of the river: Stanley Falls, Stanley Pool. Series of falls near coast, great stretches of navigable water. The proportion of the journey that could be made by water, the proportion that had to be made by land. Compare in this respect with the Mississippi and the Amazon.

3. Character of the country through which Stanley made his way: Jungle, hot, reeking with moisture, malarial. Effect on health and working capacity of explorer and his men. Compare again with Mississippi and Amazon.

4. Animals of the region—insect pests, poisonous snakes, wild animals.

5. Wild tribes, pigmies, etc., that interfered with Stanley's progress.

6. Value to the world of his expedition: Made known " Darkest Africa "; opened up trade in valuable woods, rubber, palm-oil, gums; led to building of railroad and steamboat lines; brought in Europeans with their civilizing influence (French, Belgians) thus abolishing cannibalism and greatly reducing slavery.

New England

More than half of the people of New England are engaged in manufacturing. Why?

1. Character of the country:

Surface hilly, many portions rugged, unsuited to farming on a large scale. Locate Green Mts., White Mts., Berkshires, and principal lowlands.

Effect of glacier—thin soil, rocky fields.

2. Character of rivers:

Short, shallow, interrupted by falls. Not good highways but valuable for manufacturing purposes. Lower courses only navigable. Name and locate principal rivers.

3. Character of coast:

Irregular shore-line caused by sinking of coast affords numerous good harbors. Manufactured goods may thus readily be sent out and raw material brought in. Location of principal indentations.

4. Manufacturing:

Products manufactured, sources of supply, leading centers, routes of transportation.

(1) Cotton and woolen goods (sheets, thread, dress goods, etc.). Cotton from southern states and Egypt; wool from western states and Australia. Centers: Fall River, New Bedford, Lowell, Lawrence, Manchester located on outline maps and routes traced.

(2) Leather goods (shoes, boots, etc.). Leather from West and Argentine Republic. Tanneries, where located and why. Centers: Lynn, Haverhill, Brockton located and routes traced.

(3) Watches, clocks, jewelry, etc.: Coal and iron must be imported so only small pieces of machinery are manufactured. Following cities located: Providence, jewelry; Waltham, watches; Waterbury, brass goods; New Haven, firearms.

(4) Forest products (lumber, paper, etc.): Location and extent of forests, method of lumbering, location of saw mills. Following city located: Bangor, lumber and paper.

5. Effect of manufacturing on trade:

(1) Raw materials must be brought in.

(2) Finished products must be distributed.

(3) Commodities required in the cities must be supplied, such as food, which gives rise to occupations of fishing, dairying, market-gardening; building materials, necessitating quarrying, lumbering, etc.

(4) Centers of distribution: Boston—size due to good harbor, central location in great manufacturing region, good railroad connections, etc. Providence, New Haven, Hartford, Portland, Worcester, Springfield.

III. HOME GEOGRAPHY. THE STATE OF NEW YORK

Why has New York become the Empire State?

1. Harbor: Large, deep, safe. Many miles of water front, piers and docks for ships from all over the world.
2. Hudson and Mohawk valleys: Broad Hudson, navigable for 150 miles is joined by Mohawk from the west. These two valleys form a continuous highway from the Great Lakes to the Atlantic, thus connecting New York City with the productive interior of the country.

   Importance of the Erie Canal, the New York Central and Hudson River Railroad, the Boston and Albany Railroad, etc.

   Important cities of these valleys located, their size and chief industries accounted for. Niagara Falls studied in connection with Buffalo.
3. Plateau Region (central and southern New York):

   Character of the surface, appearance of the eastern part of the plateau, the Catskills, from the Hudson Valley. Height of plateau. Sources of Delaware, Susquehanna. Why it is the farming region of the State (grapes, apples, dairy products). Compare size and number of cities in this section with those of the Hudson and Mohawk valleys.
4. Adirondack Region: Northeastern New York the highest part of the State. Mountains are well forested, beautiful lakes, fine air. Health resort. Lake Champlain and highway to Canada.

   Lumbering in this region an important industry. Wood-pulp manufactured. Many paper mills in towns along the borders of the region.
5. Highlands of the Hudson: Extend from northeast to southwest, a part of the Appalachian System. Hudson cuts through this ridge forming a wonderful water-gap. This gap is the eastern gateway of the continent and is the dominant factor in making New York the Empire State.

   Mountains here are low, forests have been largely cleared away for farms and pastures. Much valuable clay for bricks and tiles comes from this region as well as building and flag stone.

SEVENTH GRADE

I. Home Geography continued.

II. North America with special reference to United States west of Appalachians, the Dependencies of the United States, Canada, Mexico, and Central America.

III. The Asiatic countries of Japan, China, India, Russian possessions.

The selection of topics and problems for the work of the Seventh Grade is influenced by the growing intelligent interest of the pupils in world affairs and by the recent advance made by the United States as one of the dominant nations of the globe. The controlling idea is, therefore, to lead pupils to realize the great resources of our country and Canada, the opportunities offered to immigrants in the development of these resources, the consequent rapid increase in population and the westward movement of this population, the rapid growth of our cities, and the expansion of our trade relations with the Orient and with our possessions in the East.

In order to avoid the danger of trying to teach a little of everything in such a course, we focus our study upon certain important industrial sections, and teach each section as far as possible through its chief city. We study this city as the center of the industries and life of the section and discuss its relations to other cities of the United States and to cities in similar areas in other parts of the world. In this way the most important geographical features of North America are reviewed, but from a point of view very different from that followed in the early study of North America in the Fourth Grade. The geographical facts sought for and explained are those which bear directly upon the development of the city and its hinterland. In this grade as in the others, some big question or problem is generally put before the class, the solution of which gives both motive and zest for our study.

I. HOME GEOGRAPHY

We begin this study with a consideration of New York City as the greatest port in North America and as its greatest manufacturing city. The questions which direct our study are like the following:

Why has New York outdistanced all its rivals on the Atlantic Coast as a seaport?

Why should the greatest port in North America be also its greatest manufacturing center?

In solving these questions it is necessary to study about the harbor and water front of Greater New York and vicinity, its protected waterway to New England, and its water level route to the great hinterland of the Middle West. A comparison with other Atlantic seaports shows the advantages of the geographical position of New York. In considering the rapid development of manufacturing in this vicinity, we discuss the chief factors necessary for manufacturing on a large scale, *i. e.,*—ability to get hold of raw material, power, labor supply, capital, a market where the product can be sold, and transportation facilities. The kinds of manufacturing which New York has developed and its preëminence in these lines are shown to be influenced by its geographical position. Local problems, such as the necessity of improving the water front to keep pace with modern demands of commerce, and the care of the highways so that local transportation may supplement rail and water ways, are taken up as current events.

II. North America with Special Reference to United States

The chief cities studied besides New York are Pittsburgh, the industrial center of the Allegheny Plateau; New Orleans, the ocean port of the Mississippi Valley; Duluth at the head of the transportation activities of our inland seas; Minneapolis, St. Paul, and Winnipeg as the industrial and financial centers of the wheat belt; Chicago as our Inland Metropolis; Denver as leading in the activities of the Plains and Rocky Mountains; Vancouver, Seattle, and Portland as outlets of great agricultural and mining areas and as pioneers in the growing trade with China, Japan, and Alaska; San Francisco as the western gateway of our continent and the outlet of the California Valley. Some question which leads to the consideration of the Mississippi River as a whole, its peculiar features, its place as a great world river, its yet undeveloped resources as a waterway is sure to come up each year under current event topics, and to this is added as a natural consequence a study of some of the effects likely to follow the opening of the Panama Canal. The Great Plains are best studied through the Arkansas River, as it is along the rivers of this arid section that the greatest development has taken place. The series of lessons on the Great Plains given below is a type of one method of procedure in this grade.

One point emphasized in the work on the Pacific Coast cities is their outlook across the Pacific and the consequences of their growing trade with China and Japan and our Island Dependencies. It seems most fitting, therefore, that a brief study of the chief Asiatic countries should conclude the work of the year, should follow our flag, as it were, across the wide ocean that has been so long a barrier between the Eastern and Western hemispheres. No exhaustive study of these countries is attempted; our interest lies chiefly with their rebirth into the arena of world affairs, the nature and resources of each country, the characteristics of their peoples, and their possibilities for future progress along the lines of Western civilization. The topics given below under China will suggest the treatment followed with India, Japan, and the Russian possessions.

III.   Chief Countries of Asia

The chief points considered in the study of China are:

1.   Its separation in the past by land and sea from the rest of the world.

2.   That this isolation has developed in its people certain characteristics very different from those of the nations who trade with each other and travel.

3.   That China is a nation of farmers who cultivate little pieces of land and live on the produce of this land.

4.   That famines follow as a result of failure of crops and because of lack of means of communication between different sections.

5.   That seven-eighths of the 400,000,000 inhabitants are huddled into China proper.

6.   That the Chinese are industrious, patient, used to hard work, devoted to their ancestors, highly artistic, skillful, shrewd traders.

7.   That the isolation of China has been largely removed by the telegraph, steamship, and railroad, and by the efforts of the missionaries in introducing modern schools.

In discussing these points, the physical features of the country, its resources, and some of the leading cities will naturally be studied.

Before the books are closed for the year a short time is given to a comparative study of the great commercial nations of the world, of the place the United States holds among these nations, and of the reasons for the rapid development of this country in agriculture, manufacturing, and commerce.

As a result of the study here outlined we expect pupils of the Seventh Grade to know the location of certain important cities in North America as well as in the other continents, the leading industries of North America, where these are centered and why— and their influence on the distribution of population, the chief transportation routes, water and rail, and something of the influence of climate and surface on industries and life. Above all, we aim to create a real interest in geography that will not leave the pupil when he ceases to study geography as a school subject.

The following outline of a series of lessons on "The Great Plains," together with the samples of pupils' work, represents the general method of treatment in this grade.

THE GREAT PLAINS IN THEIR RELATION TO HUMAN OCCUPATION AND DEVELOPMENT

Lesson Outline

Discussion of points to be made and assignments for home lessons. General Topic and Aim:

A section of the United States known as The Great Plains was once known as The Great American Desert. To-day it is a source of great wealth and millions of people depend upon its products for food and clothing. Our purpose is to find out how it came to be thought a desert and by what means large portions have been changed to areas of great productiveness.

Where are the Great Plains? Rainfall map of United States used to fix eastern boundary, the line of 20 inches and over of rainfall per year.

How did the region come into possession of the United States? Recall Louisiana purchase. Towns already settled were St. Louis and New Orleans. Jefferson thought it wise to find out about region west of Mississippi. Children read from McMaster's "School History," page 219, about general ignorance of the government about the region.

What means did the government take to find out about this new territory? McMaster, page 330, gives routes of Lewis and Clarke's explorations, also those of Pike and Long. Major Long kept an interesting diary of his expedition.

What were some of the difficulties he would have to face?

From Longmans' Atlas, Maps 11 and 16, study general surface of country and its aridity. Dangers from scarcity of food, water, and from attacks of Indians.

Long walked 150 miles up the bed of the Arkansas River without once seeing water. In what season? Where?

In portions of stream lower down he found water holes used by buffaloes as drinking pools, but these were often muddy. Game was not abundant. Why? He finally reached the Rockies. What record on the map do we find of the accomplishment of his journey? Of Pike's expedition?

What was likely to be the nature of the report Long sent to U. S. Government? McMaster, page 331, gives a summary of Long's report. This report gave rise to the name " Great American Desert."

How would such a report affect the settlement of the region?

When gold was discovered in California and trails were blazed across this *desert* and the Rockies, the *Plains* was the most dreaded part of journey. Why?

Why did the routes of all these explorers and immigrants follow rivers?

Of the rivers the Arkansas is the most interesting and typical of a " Plains " stream. Through a study of it we shall find an answer to our question,—How has this desert been changed to an area of great productiveness?

The Arkansas is often called "The American Nile." What must be some of its characteristics?

Rises where? Fed by what? Where does it emerge from mountains? How does its character change?

Careful study of map necessary. "The Royal Gorge" is used as an illustration in some text-books. The upper portion of the river does not invite to settlement. Why? Where the river emerges on the plains there begins the agricultural development of the valley. Irrigating ditches appear east of Pueblo. At Rocky Ford are melon farms.

How do the farmers make sure of a bountiful supply of water during the summer? How are cattle and sheep watered?

The Arkansas is a strange river; the water grows less as we advance toward its mouth. In what part of the river's course does this condition begin?

The Arkansas is a two-story river. Entire stream disappears at times into the sands and reappears many miles below. Recall Long's experience. Point to a place on the map where he may have walked in the bed of the river. In March one can often walk across the bed of the river in western Kansas and eastern Colorado. A half mile of level sand with the narrow ribbon of the stream winding across it is all that lies under the long bridges that span the Arkansas. (Dodge's Advanced Geography, page 25, has a picture of the braided channels of the Platte.)

When might this narrow stream become a flood? (Recall when snows on the mountains melt.)

Some one has said that the Arkansas is 2.000 miles long, half a mile wide, and six inches deep. Which of these dimensions is constant?

The early emigrants who followed the Platte and Arkansas suffered terrible hardships from lack of water. Yet there was water if they had known where to find it.

Where did Long find it? Through what kind of soil must stream flow through for this to happen? What should cause the stream to rise to surface again?

Settlers afterward bored for water; sometimes they found it at a few feet, sometimes hundreds, below the surface.

Where does the force come from that makes the well spout?

Sometimes the water must be pumped. On the Great Plains windmills pump water onto the land. In what country do windmills pump water out of the land? The windmill is a feature of all farms.

Compare the artesian well with the water hole of the buffalo. How has it been possible to turn this so-called desert into sheep and cattle ranches and melon farms? Locate the grazing section of the Great Plains.

In the lower portion of river's course the stream comes permanently to the surface and behaves as a normal river should. (Use rainfall map to determine where this will be.) Here the plains merge into the prairies and farming is not confined to the river valleys, nor dependent on underground waters for supply.

What are the occupations and industries of the dwellers on the Plains?

Map 17 of Longmans' Atlas shows grazing areas. The extension of irrigation products and the introduction of "dry farming" bring every year more land under cultivation. There are few large cities. Denver and Pueblo at the western boundary, Wichita at the eastern are flourishing towns. The products of the ranches are shipped east. To what point in Nebraska? in Missouri? in Illinois? To what industries in these cities do these products give rise? What railroad lines cross these states? Which of them follow routes of explorers? Which follows the old Santa Fé trail?

Many boys and girls brought up in the Plains have never seen a lake, a river, perhaps not even a tree, yet they have many comforts of modern life. Do you think they have telephone service and Rural Free Delivery on the steppes of Russia or the Plains of Hungary or Argentine?

Compare these areas for products, language spoken, lines of transportation, cities.

Assignments for Home Lessons

1. On an outline map of United States color the Great Plains section, write names of states wholly or partly in the Plains, and the names of rivers which cross them. Learn these facts.

2. Add routes of explorers with dates.

3. Write a description of the Arkansas as a two-story river.

4. Draw a series of illustrations with explanatory notes showing the source of underground water, an artesian well, a windmill pumping water for stock, a sketch map of the Arkansas River.

5. Use your text-book and be prepared on the industries of the Great Plains, the location of cities, and transportation routes.

6. Place the facts learned in Exercise 5 on an outline map of the United States.

7. Use your text-book and find out all you can about the steppes of Russia and the Plains of Hungary and Argentine. Write these facts in three paragraphs.

8. Bring in a written report of the class lesson of to-day.

Pupil's Work Illustrating Some of the Above Assignments. Written Report of Class Lesson of Previous Day

The Great Plains of America

What are the boundaries?

The western boundary is the Rocky Mountains, the eastern boundary the twenty-inch rainfall line.

How did we acquire it?

From France, as the Louisiana Territory, omitting Texas, in 1803.

How did President Jefferson know about it?

He sent out an expedition, to explore the country, headed by Major Long.

What were the two cities?

New Orleans and St. Louis.

Was the journey to be easy or hard? Why?

Hard. Because they had to depend on what they caught for provisions, and perhaps have attacks from the Indians.

What was the route and season?

The season was spring. He started at St. Louis, went up the Missouri, the Kansas and the Arkansas Rivers.

Where is his name commemorated?

At Long's Peak.

What was his report?

Region much like Sahara Desert.

How did they come to be called the Great Desert of America?

From the reports of Pike and Long.

When did the first rush of population cross them?

In 1849, to California, for gold.

SKETCHES AND MAP PREPARED AS HOME WORK

THE GREAT PLAINS.

ROCKIES.

INDIANS
STOPPING
COMMERCE

GREAT PLAINS

As It Was

FARMS.

CITY.

COMMERCE.

As It Is Now.

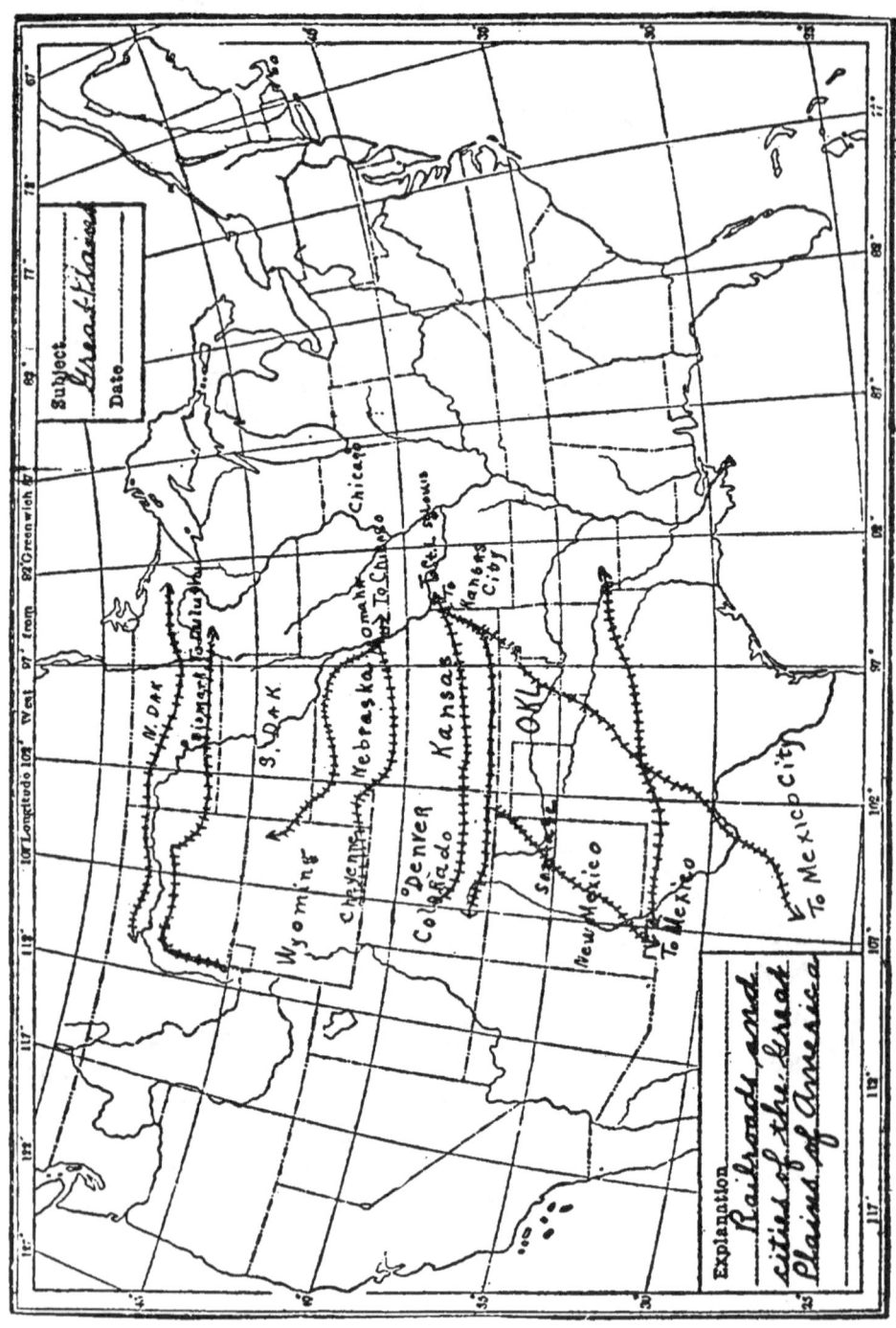

Railroads and cities of the Great Plains of America

STUDY OF NEW YORK CITY

The purpose of this study of New York is to acquaint the children with their own city, to interest them in the efforts of its best citizens toward a higher ideal of city life and government, and to inspire them with a desire to do something for their city. This knowledge should include (1) the actual physical features of the city; (2) the inhabitants, their number and nationality; (3) the occupations of the people and some of the problems arising on account of the industrial pursuits in which many of them are engaged; (4) some of the institutions aiming to solve the most pressing of these problems, *viz.*, the Consumer's League, the Child Labor organizations, the City Club; (5) the history of New York and historic spots in the city; (6) the beautiful things in New York, buildings, parks, museums, art collections, etc.; (7) the means for protecting life and property, *viz.*, the Police and Fire departments, courts.

As will be seen by consulting the tabulated outline below, the method of presenting these topics and questions is to draw from each subject of the curriculum any material which may apply to New York, rather than to organize a special course not related to all school subjects. The time schedule is not necessarily fixed, but each phase of the study is taken up in the natural setting of the general course from which it is drawn. The amount of time given to this study varies from two to four weeks, according to the grade of the child and the subject under consideration. A more detailed treatment of these topics is given in other parts of the course of study under the general heading at the top of each column.

STUDY OF

RADES	HISTORY AND CIVICS	GEOGRAPHY	FINE ARTS
VII	Political divisions of city Industrial protection Comparison with the past Dep'ts of City Government and their work	New York as a port, as a manufacturing center Streets, plan of city Terminals — water — rail	Civic art Improvement of city
VI	United States history Discoveries Colonial history	New York State and Hudson River	Some works of art in New York. Examples of Colonial art
V	United States post-office. Its work in the city. Comparison with mediaeval times.	Foreign population Immigration	Tiffany glass. Collections of pottery and porcelain in museums, shops.
IV	Police protection Comparison with the past	Transportation and communication Streets Tunnels Bridges	Study of collections of textiles and plates in Metropolitan Museum. Design work. Appearance of city street compared with country road.
III	Early history Fire protection	Surface of city — map of New York Continuation of weather study	Sunny, grey, and stormy days along the Hudson Firemen in action
II	Early history		

NEW YORK CITY

INDUSTRIAL ARTS	SCIENCE	LITERA-TURE	HOUSEHOLD ARTS
Wood, steel, cement and metal industries of New York; the various phases and importance of these industries from a social and economic viewpoint.		Local poets and writers	Cooking Food inspec Pure food la
	Water supply of New York	Irving	Colonial indust Textiles Garment-mak-ing Industrial an social pro lems
	Forestry Trees and birds of parks		
	Sources of food, clothing, shelter: sugar fibres tea rubber fish building- lumber stones	Stories of inventors, engineers, builders	
Shelter, food, clothing Brick-making Milk supply Wool market	Vegetable gardens Shrubs Vines } of parks Flowers Beaver Sea-gull		
Work illustrating occupations of Indians on Manhattan Island Clays Textiles	Native plants and animals Weather Rain Snow Temperature Evaporation		

HISTORY

The present course of study in history presents many modifications of the course published six years ago. We have been and still are trying out new ideas both as to subject matter and method, so that the outline offered here is not final, but represents what at the present time seems best adapted to the particular needs of our pupils.

The work of the earlier grades cannot with exactness be called history. In the First Grade, for instance, it is rather a study of sociology, putting the children into intelligent connection with their surroundings. From a study of the home they are led out through the work of the father into a larger environment to observe those who are occupied in providing them with the necessities of life. To emphasize the universality of the family idea, sharply contrasting homes from other parts of the world are brought in, the homes of the Dutch and the Eskimo.

In the work of the Second Grade there enter certain large historical concepts. The elements of time and change are introduced at this point, when the children are taken back three hundred years to a study of Manhattan Island with its Indian inhabitants. Here two sets of conditions far apart in time are brought in for comparison to develop these concepts.

In the Third Grade, with the discoveries of Hudson, still another element is involved, that of movement. For the first time a logical succession of events, each depending on the preceding, is presented. We chose this material because local history always contains a natural interest and reality for little folk, and because so large an amount of matter was readily accessible.

The study of New York is followed by that of colonial New England, where we see the transplanted English develop into Americans, illustrating the changes wrought in a people by the action of their surroundings,—a fourth important historical concept.

In the reorganized course of history, the work of the Fourth

Grade is not sufficiently worked out to give more than a general statement. In this year we take up the Greeks and early Romans, beginning with their story as it emerges from legend into authentic history, and bringing it down to the time when Greece becomes a Roman province. Very little time will be spent on wars, etc., but we plan to emphasize such topics as will build up very concrete notions of what Greek life really was like, and to give some of their beliefs as expressed in myths.

The presentation of historical epochs in their sequence begins in the Fifth Grade with the study of Roman history and the Middle Ages. From there on the evolution of events is followed consecutively in the Sixth and Seventh Grades. The Sixth Grade makes a study of the European background of American history, and follows the course of American history to the close of the Revolution, while the Seventh Grade continues the development of the United States up to the present day.

In assigning the study of the Greeks to the Fourth Grade it was necessary to move backward the subject matter of the three following years. This adjustment allows us time to bring United States history down to our day, giving an opportunity for the consideration of such questions as the colonization and development of our West, and the United States as a world power with its attendant responsibilities.

Besides this shifting of material, there is throughout the course a noteworthy tendency to cut down the number of topics, allowing more time to those we consider more worth while. The outline as printed may be somewhat misleading in this respect, but several points included are touched on just enough to keep the connection between the subjects of greater importance. In the treatment of wars this is especially true. While we have not *entirely* reached a peace basis and do not intend to eliminate war altogether, we have cut out many of the actual military operations, putting the emphasis rather on causes and results. However, we do believe there is a legitimate place for some of the stirring tales of battles and military heroes. Aside from their knowledge as a matter of information, the love of the dramatic in the normal boy and girl furnishes sufficient reason for including these thrilling stories.

The condensation referred to above leaves us free to devote

ourselves more exclusively to matters of social and industrial importance. So, as historians furnish us more and more authentic information regarding the common things of former times, we are able increasingly to emphasize those concrete matters which are most interesting to young folks, how people ate, slept, travelled and conducted themselves generally. As each year adds to the mass of historical source material adaptable to elementary work, we increasingly avail ourselves of this means to put our classes into more vital connection with the past.

In American history especially there are many of the more important documents available for class-room use. By referring to an excellent facsimile of the Declaration of Independence, we can give our pupils a vivid summary of the colonists' grievances against King George as stated by the revolutionists themselves, also the date, the place of assembling, how the Congress was made up, etc. And when the students see the broad signature of Hancock, and the queer cramped writing of the other signers, they do not soon forget who was president of the Congress and what men took that decisive step.

Pictures also form most excellent source material for work with young folks. While formerly about the only sort of illustration a history teacher could muster was a fanciful General Putnam galloping gaily down a stairway pursued by the British, we are at present supplied with authentic illustrations for all periods. Just as Alice Morse Earle has made vivid the everyday life of our colonial ancestors, so Mau has pictured for us how the old Roman ground his flour and baked his bread. Then, too, the Sunday newspapers and illustrated magazines furnish much illustrative material. At the time of the Lincoln Centenary a few years ago, we were able to collect quite a complete set of reprints and photographs representing the life of that president.

Another tendency in method which has been influencing our history teaching more and more is due to our conviction that, while giving attention to things ancient, we must arouse and keep alive the feeling in the pupils that all this is of real concern to them. Consequently, whenever it can profitably be done, connection is made between the lesson and present-day conditions. This has the twofold value of giving perspective to the life of the present, while at the same time vivifying a far-off event. When the latter is too remote, the teacher bides her time until the chain of events shall bring the matter near enough for the comparison to be natural, always taking care not to warp facts to fit a theory. This method lends itself most readily to modern history.

It so happens that we begin the study of the Constitution about the first of December, when the newspapers are giving considerable space to the assembling of Congress and its doings. So the class gathers its ideas of the working of the Constitution through watching how a live congress conducts itself, and what a president actually does. During the six months following, nearly all the powers of both branches of Congress will be brought into play, and the executive called on to perform most of the duties allotted him. This sort of work, aside from the interest created, leaves the desired impression that the Constitution is not an uninteresting document concocted by our ancestors a hundred years ago, but a vital instrument affecting our life of to-day.

While events of American history are more easily put in connection with modern times than the more ancient, still there are many points of contact to be found with the earlier periods. The guilds of the Middle Ages, for instance, are not so unlike our labor unions of to-day, even to the boycott method of bringing the employers to terms. And back in Imperial Rome the natatorium with its underground heating apparatus bears a strong resemblance to the swimming tank of our own school.

Another modification since our last published account is the increased time devoted to current events, especially in the Seventh Grade. Through this we try to awaken a lively interest in history in the making. We endeavor to train pupils to cull from the mass of news that which is of lasting interest and which bears on great movements. Aside from the main object of such work, there are several by-products. One of the most valuable is the light it throws on the past. In following the evolution of the aeroplane, for instance, the boy compares it with that of the steamboat and locomotive, realizing that these inventions also were the results of slow growth and did not spring " full-armed " into being. These current events are often utilized as a starting point for a series of lessons in geography, as in the study of Central America—part of the prescribed course in geography—

the approach was made through an interest awakened in the Panama Canal. So, also, the political situation in the Balkans this year has furnished a natural introduction into the required review of Europe.

We find this also affords excellent matter for oral English lessons. From the wide range of subjects offered, the pupil selects what to him appears of paramount interest and importance, leading him naturally to express himself with force and conciseness.

The following is an outline of the topics planned for the various grades beginning with the fall of 1913.

FIRST GRADE

Study of Home and Environment

I. The home as a center. An enlargement of work already done in kindergarten.

   1. Occupations of members of the family.

   2. A consideration of the service that father renders the community leads the child to a study of the occupations that contribute to the obvious needs of the house, especially those that provide food and clothing. Emphasis on the idea of interdependence.

   3. Excursions to a general farm in New Jersey in the fall when crops are being harvested, also to a market.

   4. Lessons based on excursions. Pupils list middle-men between farmer and consumer to get the idea of the long chain of people concerned in bringing food to their homes.

   5. Thanksgiving, the culmination of the harvest, is brought out in songs and stories.

   6. A farm is constructed on the sand table. Pictures of farms, markets, etc., are brought by the children and used to illustrate the reading book which is a summary of the fall's work.

   7. Some of the occupations that furnish woolen, cotton, and silk clothing to the family. The workers concerned in the production of these are listed to give

the class an idea of the chain of men engaged in serving them.

II. Illustrative material. Simple weaving.
   1. Simpler homes from different parts of the world compared with ours, emphasizing the universal relationships.
   2. Excursion to Natural History Museum to study Eskimo exhibit.
   3. Illustrative material: Eskimo village built on sand table.

III. Stories from primitive life told to emphasize the simpler phases of family life.

IV. Miniature home made by class, with suitable furniture.

V. Return to the work of the farm in the spring to complete the observations made in the fall. This also forms a basis for the season's work in nature-study.

SECOND GRADE

EARLY LIFE ON MANHATTAN ISLAND

I. Immediate neighborhood.
   1. Changes constantly taking place here.
   2. Picture island before 1609.
   3. Use descriptions, models, pictures.

II. The Indians.
   1. How we know they were here. Excursions to Natural History Museum. Late discoveries found here.
   2. Study of the Indians themselves. Appearance, clothing, food, shelter, occupations, games.
   3. Stories the Indians told about themselves.

III. Henry Hudson and the Dutch.
   1. Hudson's discovery.
      (a) Motive.
      (b) Description of boat.
      (c) Arrival in New York Harbor.
      (d) Trip up the Hudson.
      (e) Result of discovery.
   2. Establishment of New Amsterdam.

References :

Smithsonian Reports.
Dutch Village Communities on the Hudson River, Elting of Johns Hopkins.
Old South Leaflets, No. 69. Van der Douk's description of New Netherlands, 1655.
Manhattan Island and Its Inhabitants.
Historical Inquiry Concerning Henry Hudson, Read, Albany 1866.
Old Indian Legends Retold, Zetkala.
Indian Myths, Emerson.
Story of Manhattan, Charles Hemstat.
New Amsterdam and Its People, J. H. Innes.

THIRD GRADE

Colonial History

I. Early New York.
    1. Review New York history given in Second Grade.
    2. Life in New Amsterdam.
        (a) Homes.
        (b) Clothing.
        (c) Food.
        (d) Occupations.
        (e) Education.
        (f) Governor Stuyvesant.
    3. One of the great estates.
    4. Reference made to the English conquest and the Revolution.

II. Life in Massachusetts.
    1. Plymouth Plantation.
        (a) Motive for founding colony.
        (b) Voyage.
        (c) Planting colony.
        (d) Life under Governor Bradford.
        (e) Industries developed.
        (f) Comparison with life in New York.

III. Life in Virginia.
    1. Motive for settlement.
    2. John Smith and his experiences.
    3. Later life on a plantation.

IV. Men commemorated by our national holidays.
    1. Columbus.
    2. Washington.
    3. Lincoln.

REFERENCES:

Child Life in Colonial Days, Earle.
Home Life in Colonial Days, Earle.
Colonial Days in Old New York, Earle.
Colonial Children, Hart.
Industrial Evolution of the United States, Wright.
Dutch Village Communities on the Hudson River, Elting of Johns
   Hopkins.
A Landmark History of New York, Ullman.
Plymouth Plantation, Bradford.
Massachusetts Historical Collection, Series IV, Vol. III.
Customs of Old New England, Earle.
Pilgrims and Puritans, Tiffany.
Economic History of New England, Weeden.
Beginnings of New England, Fiske.
Adrian Block, Smith and Perry.
A True Relation, Capt. John Smith.
American History Leaflet, No. 27.
Colonial Cavalier, Goodwin.
Stories of the Old Dominion, Cooke.
Knights of the Golden Horseshoe, Cooke.
Virginia, Cooke.

FOURTH GRADE

GREEK AND EARLY ROMAN HISTORY

The outline for this grade has not yet been worked out, but
when finished will include such topics as: the wide distribution
of the Greeks, geographical conditions affecting their life,
customs in common, the Olympian Games, etc., life of a Spartan
family, of an Athenian family in the Age of Pericles, some of
their religious beliefs as expressed in their myths. A similar
treatment will be given the Early Roman period.

FIFTH GRADE

ROMAN HISTORY AND MIDDLE AGES

I. Rome extends her conquests beyond Italy.
    1. War with Macedonia and Greece.
    2. War with Antiochus and Mithridates.

II. Civil strife in Rome.
1. The Gracchi.
2. Marius and Sulla.
3. Caesar and Pompey.

III. Rome as an Empire.
1. Julius Caesar.
2. The reign of Augustus. Roman life at that time:
(a) Homes.
(b) Dress.
(c) Schools.
(d) Writers.
(e) Buildings.
(f) Life of the Forum.
3. Extent of empire, 14 A. D.

IV. Influence of Roman civilization on subsequent history.
1. Laws.
2. Calendars, numerals, names of months.

V. Ancient Germans.
1. Manner of life compared with American Indians.
2. Characteristics of people.
3. Location of principal tribes.
4. Relations with the Romans.

VI. Breaking up of the Roman Empire. The barbaric invasions affecting the life of the people. Emphasis on:
1. Invasion of Angles and Saxons.
(a) Condition of Britain under Romans.
(b) Cause of invasion.
(c) Character of invaders.
(d) King Alfred.
2. Invasion of Franks.
(a) Reason for their strength.
(b) Clovis.
(c) Charlemagne.
(d) Why their power lasted.

3. Norsemen.
   (a) Location.
   (b) Character.
   (c) Conquest of France.
   (d) Conquest of England.

VII. Feudalism and Chivalry.
   1. Feudalism as a way of governing.
      (a) The importance of owning land.
      (b) What a vassal owed to his lord.
   2. Chivalry.
      (a) What a knight vowed.
      (b) Ceremonies attending knighting a squire.

VIII. Mohammedanism.
   1. Mohammed and his teachings.
   2. Invasion of Mohammedans.

IX. Life in Middle Ages.
   1. In the castle.
   2. In the monastery.
   3. In the village.
   4. In the town.

REFERENCES:

Roman Period
   Text-Book: Story of the Romans, Guerber.
   Story of Rome as the Greeks and Romans Tell It, Botsford.
   Pompeii, Its Life and Art, Mau.
   Studies in Greek and Roman History, Sheldon.
   Iliad, Bryant's translation.
   Plutarch's Lives.
   Letters of Caius Plinius Caecilius Secundus, translated by Melmoth.
   History of Rome, Botsford.

Middle Ages
   Text-Book: A Story of the Middle Ages, Harding.
   Introduction to Middle Ages, Emerton.
   History of Western Europe, Robinson.
   Germania, Tacitus.
   Chronicles, Froissart.
   Readings in European History, Robinson.
   Mediaeval Civilization, Adams.

SIXTH GRADE

EUROPEAN BEGINNINGS OF AMERICAN HISTORY
AMERICAN HISTORY THROUGH THE REVOLUTION

I. The Church.
II. The Crusades.
1. Conditions which led to these.
2. Main points to be considered in the First Crusade.
3. How the Third Crusade differed from the First.
4. Peculiarities of the Fourth Crusade.
5. Economic and political results of the Crusades.
III. King John and The Magna Charta.
1. How King John helped to develop a love of liberty in English hearts.
2. What was done to bring the King to a realization of his obligations.
3. Provisions of the Magna Charta.
IV. The Hundred Years' War.
1. Causes.
2. Periods of the War.
3. Results.
V. Civilization of Western Europe in Middle Ages.
1. Appearances of cities.
(a) What streets were like.
(b) Ideas of cleanliness and sanitation held at that time.
(c) Public buildings: cathedrals, guildhalls, town halls.
2. Clothing of people.
(a) Costumes of noblemen, monks, peasants, merchants, jesters.
(b) Where the materials came from.
3. Armor and weapons.
4. Method of distinguishing one iron-clad man from another.
VI. The revival of learning.
1. Search for old manuscripts.
2. Study of Greek.

      3. Great authors of that time.

      4. Paintings of Michael Angelo, Raphael.

      5. Important inventions:

         (a) Gunpowder and cannon.

         (b) Compass.

         (c) Paper made from linen.

VII. Printing—movable type.

      1. John Gutenburg, William Caxton, Erasmus.

      2. Books first printed.

VIII. Discovery of America.

      1. Notions of size and shape of earth:

         (a) Maps.

         (b) Distribution of land and water.

      2. Trade with East at end of Middle Ages.

      3. More correct knowledge of earth.

      4. Race for the Indies by Spain and Portugal.

      5. Voyages of Columbus.

      6. What Spain and Portugal did to make good their claims.

IX. Exploration of America.

      1. Questions still unsolved by voyages.

      2. Famous explorers: Cortez, Coronado, LaSalle.

X. England in the time of Henry VIII.

      1. Character of Henry.

      2. His quarrel with the Pope.

      3. Attitude toward the mediæval church in other countries.

XI. England under Queen Elizabeth.

XII. The planting of American colonies. Review of Third Grade work.

XIII. Government of Colonies.

      1. Who chose governor, customs officers, judges.

      2, Where money came from to pay these officials.

XIV. Commerce.

      1. Main routes.

      2. Products exchanged.

XV.   King George attempts to bring the Colonists under stricter control.
1.   Navigation laws, when enforced, interfere with commerce.
2.   Tea Tax—Boston Port Bill.
3.   Transportation of Americans to England for trial.

XIV.   Armed resistance to King George.
1.   Preparation for war.
2.   Outbreak in Massachusetts.
   (a)   Lexington, Concord, Bunker Hill.
   (b)   Washington in command.
3.   Campaign at the center.   Study of this in detail.
4.   Declaration of Independence.
5.   History of our flag.
6.   George Rogers Clarke and the Northwest Territory.
7.   Adventures of John Paul Jones.
8.   Campaign in the South.   Very brief.
9.   King George recognizes our independence and acknowledges our right to land east of Mississippi River.

REFERENCES:

Text-Books: European Beginnings of American History, Atkinson.
A History of the United States, Thwaites and Kendall.
For Middle Ages and period of colonization
Source Book of Mediaeval History, Ogg.
English History Told by the English Poets, Bates and Comens.
The Boys' Froissart.
Readings in European History, Robinson.
Readings in English History, Cheyney.
Studies in American History, Sheldon Barnes.
American History Told by Contemporaries, Hart.
Source Book, Hart.
Old South Leaflets.
Letters of Washington.
Samuel Sewell's Diary.
Book of American Explorers, Higginson.
Struggle for a Continent, Parkman.
The American Revolution, Fiske.
A Critical History of the United States, Winson.
Industrial Evolution of the United States, Carroll Wright.

SEVENTH GRADE

UNITED STATES HISTORY FROM THE CLOSE OF THE REVOLUTION TO THE PRESENT TIME

I. Weak national government results in:
    1. Trouble between states.
    2. Lack of funds.

II. Growth of union sentiment.
    1. Northwest Territory.
    2. Constitution adopted. Study of national government.

III. Starting governmental machinery.
    1. Inauguration of Washington.
    2. Cabinet.
    3. Matters to be settled.
    4. Formation of political parties.

IV. Foreign relations adjusted with:
    1. France.
    2. Barbary States.
    3. England.
    4. Spain, Russia.
        (a) Monroe Doctrine.
        (b) Florida.

V. Westward expansion.
    1. Louisiana Territory. Lewis and Clarke's expedition.
    2. Improvements in transportation leading to colonization of West.
        (a) National Road.
        (b) Steamboats.
        (c) Canals.
        (d) Railroads.
    3. Western states admitted as a result.
    4. Reaction on eastern cities.
    5. Jackson, our first western president. A type.
        (a) Spoils system.

VI. Slavery and its results.
1. Opinion of Washington, Clay and others on slavery.
2. Picture of plantation life in Virginia, in South Carolina.
3. Cotton gin and steam machinery creates increased demand for slaves.
4. Keeping balance between North and South.
    (a) Missouri Compromise.
    (b) Acquisition of Texas.
    (c) Mexican secession.
    (d) Kansas-Nebraska trouble.
    (e) California.
5. Dred Scott case.
6. John Brown.
7. Secession, and formation of Confederacy.
8. Civil War.
    (a) Comparison of strength of North and South.
    (b) Object and result of campaigns. Battles of Vicksburg and Gettysburg in detail.
    (c) Emancipation Proclamation.
9. Sherman's march to the sea.
10. Surrender of southern armies.
11. Reconstruction.
    (a) Officers and army of the South.
    (b) Slaves in loyal states.
    (c) Southern debt.
    (d) Seceding states.
    (e) Amendments to Constitution.

VII. Expansion and development since the War.
1. Acquisition of Alaska, Hawaii.
2. Discovery of gold in the Rockies, with resulting emigration.
3. Development of West encouraged by Congress.
    (a) Homestead Act.
    (b) Charters to transcontinental railroads.
    (c) Immigration laws.

(d) Irrigation systems established.

(e) Indian reservations.

(f) Control of railroads, Interstate Commerce Act, Railway Rate Act.

4. States formed along route of transcontinental railroads.

5. Help from Department of Agriculture.

6. Improvements in communication.

(a) Cables and telegraphs.

(b) Post office: rural free delivery; parcel post.

(c) Telephones.

7. Foreign relations.

(a) War with Spain. United States becomes a world power.

(b) Relations with China and Japan.

(c) Arbitration treaties and Hague tribunal

(d) Immigration.

VIII. Civil Government of New York City.

REFERENCES:

Text-Book: A History of the United States, Thwaites and Kendall.
Letters of Washington.
Old South Leaflets.
American History Leaflets.
Source Book, Hart.
Studies in American History, Sheldon Barnes.
Autobiography of Franklin.
Story of the Atlantic Cable, Cyrus Field.
Historic Highways, Hulburt.
Abraham Lincoln—A History, Nicolay Hay.
From Trail to Railway, Brigham.
Social Life in Old Virginia, Page.
The Westward Movement, Winson.
Critical Period of American History, Fiske.
Mississippi River in the Civil War, Fiske.
Parley's Reminiscences of Sixty Years in the National Capital.

MUSIC

The plan for the music of the elementary grades is based upon "Education Through Music"' by Professor Farnsworth of Teachers College. The work is divided into three groups: From Song to Notation, Grades 1-3; from Notation to Song, Grades 4-6; Broadening Musical Experience, Grades 7-8.

FIRST AND SECOND PHASES

The first phase, From Song to Notation, presents the work through a direct musical appeal. The pupil is led to observe, define, and finally describe in terms of musical notation what, in all cases, he has first heard and sung. Musical experience in the form of rote songs is given and this experience is gradually defined through association with notation. The child passes from expression through imitation, to thought. Drill grows out of the effort to formulate what is felt.

The second phase, From Notation to Song, complements the first in that the process is reversed and the musical thought is first presented to the eye in notation. This the pupil rapidly coördinates, forming a musical concept which he finally sings. Drill in the practical application of the association formed by means of sight-singing is emphasized. The child passes from thought through notation to expression. Drill grows out of the effort to formulate what is seen.

The first and second phases taken together supply the musical experience, knowledge, and skill necessary to form the basis of the third and last phase of the work.

THIRD PHASE

The third phase has for its aim not so much the development of technical skill as the widening of musical experience and knowledge by interesting the pupils in instruments, instrumental music, its forms and characteristics, and musical biography and history.

64

As any plan must be adapted to conditions under which it is to be used, we have found it necessary to adapt and cut down the work advised by Professor Farnsworth for pupils above the primary grades, so as to conform to the limited time schedule of the Fifth to the Seventh grades,—the time per week being as follows: Fifth Grade, two fifteen-minute class-room periods and one twenty-minute chorus period; Sixth Grade, one twenty-minute class-room and one twenty-minute chorus period; Seventh Grade, one twenty-five minute chorus period.

Believing that good tone, clear enunciation and imaginative singing are essential to any degree of beauty in singing, and also necessary as a foundation for musical experience upon which to base the technique of sight-reading, we have aimed first to lead the children to imagine vividly, enunciate clearly and sing with good tone,—all this as outlined in " Education Through Music." The plan of work for drill in the technique of sight-reading we have carried out in Grades I to IV. However, in Grades V to VII, the time for class-room lessons has not been sufficient to enable us to accomplish all the drill in technique. While aiming to retain what has been gained in beauty in singing, we are giving these pupils a general knowledge of musical notation, as outlined, sacrificing somewhat the drill in sight-reading for the sake of more singing of good songs. A wider choice of songs is made possible by aiding the pupils when necessary in the difficult parts of songs, thus preserving the freshness of the songs and also saving time for more effective drill in the artistic expression of what is sung. Pupils are encouraged to sing alone from memory songs that will be valuable after school days.

In time, we aim to give the drill required for the three grades included in " From Notation to Song." This will enable us to begin in the Seventh Grade what is outlined for " Broadening Musical Experience."

The choice of subjects for study and drill grows out of the nature of the child and the relation to each other of the musical problems to be solved. These problems are dealt with in stages, each having a characteristic feature, *e. g.,* tone-production, rhythm, pitch. These again are divided into steps, when necessary, each stage or step taking from three to six weeks, sufficiently long to complete a unit of work and to make a definite lasting impression that may be built upon when the subjects recur and yet not long enough to weary the pupil, destroying interest.

LIST OF STAGES, STEPS AND SONGS

In the following outlines the formal work necessarily occupies the most space, but actual practice through emphasis on song singing keeps the balance between the two kinds of work.

First Phase, First Year. Awakening Musical Ideas: (1) Rhythmic interest in the song, supplying a means for all to join, even those who are too shy to sing. (2) Voice—improvement in tone and pronunciation through the efforts to express adequately the thought of the song. Helping monotones to find their singing voices. (3) Observation of the character of the song through attempts to act and picture the way it goes with reference to pitch, duration, pulse. (4) Learning key relationship of tones by singing syllable names as another stanza to simple songs, such as " Hot Cross Buns." (5) Playing " Echo " and imitating musical sounds for the purpose of developing control of breath and tone quality.

First Phase, Second Year. Defining musical ideas and beginning to express them by means of notation. Defining Interpretation and Structural Ideas: (1) Voice work: Good position of body. Good breath control. The vowel, the thread upon which the tone is sung. All developed from effort to make the song sound better. (2) Key quality. Observing through song sentences the characteristic effects produced by each of the seven tones of the key and associating the sound names and hand signs with the tones they represent, establishing the third and fifth as initial tones, followed by scale practice. (3) Tone duration: Combining the acting and picturing of pulse and duration, thus learning how to measure tones of different lengths—quarters, halves, eighths. (4) Simplified notation: Discovering the advantages of lines in representing differences in pitch and learning how to write measured music upon them. (5) Practice in finding rapidly the third and fifth on the staff. (6) Song-making: Learning how a musical passage of four or five notes sounds from the way it looks and how to form and express our own tonal thoughts by song making.

First Phase, Third Year. Completion of the process from song to notation and commencing phrase reading: (1) Review of notation learned in second year; continuation of the work through appeal to the imagination. Specific vowel practice on sustained tones. (2) Completion of staff notation. First step: Learning to sing major and minor seconds at will in order to be able to measure staff distances. Second step: Discovering the need for fixed pitch as well as relative names of tones, learning how the fixed pitch names came to be, and how to sing them starting from any one of them. Third step: Learning how the clef mark makes it possible to have the lines of the staff represent fixed pitches and how to sing them from the staff. Fourth step: Discovering how the staff with the clef mark can represent only the key of C and how sharps and flats are made to represent other keys. (3) Fractional pulse: Observing the difference between the dotted pulse and the dotted half pulse and memorizing their effect as well as learning how they are represented in notation. (4) Phrase thinking: Inventing variations on a musical passage and writing them down, as well as continuing song-making. (5) Commencing phrase reading in the three keys, C, F, G.

Second Phase, Fourth Year. Beginning of the work from Notation to Song and development of phrase reading. (1) Continned practice of good voice and vowel color through efforts to express adequately the character of the song. (2) Thinking music in phrases; singing and writing variations on a phrase. (3) Speed work; practice in rapid coördination by pointing on staff without writing, and by use of printed cards. Application of phrase practice to songs. (4) Learning new keys; applying the observation with reference to the sharp four and flat seven as a principle for introducing new keys and forming key groups. Rhythmic practice. (5) Speed work in placing 1st, 3rd, upper and lower 5th, and upper octave in different keys. (6) Introduction of musical reader.

Second Phase, Fifth Year. Continuation of the work from Notation to Song: (1) Continuation of the phrase reading begun in the fourth year, practiced in connection with song work. Gradual increase in the difficulty of phrases used, and shortening of the time allowed for observing. The use of minor phrases upon which to write variations. Continuation of the same attention to means of interpretation employed in the previous grades. (2) Fundamentals of good tone studied as such: ·(a) Breath, deep and free, controlled by the muscles about the waist. (b) Loose and flexible muscles about the neck and mouth. (c) Resonant body, especially chest and head. (d) The recognition and use of head tones. (e) Learning a classified list of good singing vowels. (3) Development of the minor mode. Giving experience of minor tones, observing and describing what makes them sound as they do. Learning how to sing the new tones. Practice on the harmonic and melodic forms of the minor scales and chords. (4) Speed work in recognition of key-signatures. (5) Continuation of work in readers.

Second Phase, Sixth Year. Completion of the process from Notation to Song: (1) Continuation throughout the year of sight-singing. Practice in recognizing phrase groups, as well as phrases. (2) Study of chords; more systematic practice of part singing. The observation of tones sounded together. The discovery of the principal chords, their inversions and how they succeed each other, practice in learning to recognize and name them. The work under this head divided into several periods. (3) Learning the key groups. Observing the change of keys that takes place in many tunes. Classifying these changes and learning the chromatic marks that indicate each change. (4) Speed work in naming degrees of staff and relating scale names to them in different keys.

Third Phase, Seventh Year.[1] Work for broadening and deepening universal interest: (1) Song practice not only for the purpose of technical drill but also for the sake of getting acquainted with good literature, and for supplying material for school music functions. (2) Awakening interest in instruments: (a) Observing instruments. (b) Learning about bands and orchestras and the value of knowing how to play band instruments. (3) Awakening interest in instrumental music, especially that of the march and dance forms, used by bands. Observing the relation of the dance to music, how it punctuates the music. Learning some of the historic origins of the dance forms.

---

[1] For the completion of the work in the eighth grade and for the plan of all the grades in detail see " Education Through Music."

Song Material

We are using "Songs for Schools" with its supplement for our general assembly singing. A partial list of the songs contained in this collection is given below.

The choice of song material, especially in the earlier grades, grows out of the seasonal changes of the year, special programs, and the recurring festivals, such as Thanksgiving, Christmas and May Day.

The following list of songs is classified in three divisions, A, B, and C. A indicates short, easy songs of small range, suitable for Grades I and II; B, longer or more difficult songs suitable for Grades III and IV; C, songs still more difficult or of still wider range, suitable for Grades V to VII.

The page numbers are given and, in a few cases, changes in key or words are suggested.

Songs for Schools, C. H. Farnsworth. Macmillan.

Songs of the British Isles, W. H. Hadow. Novello.

The Children's Messiah, Marie Ruef Hofer. , Clayton F. Summy Co.

Rounds, Carols and Songs, Margaret Cushing Osgood—Oliver Ditson Co.

Nature Songs for Children, Fanny Knowlton. Milton Bradley Co.

Art Song Cycles—Part I, Miessner. Silver Burdett.

Song Year Book, Helen Place. Silver Burdett.

Small Songs for Small Singers, W. H. Neidlinger. G. Schirmer.

Songs and Games for Little Ones, Walker and Jenks. Oliver Ditson Co.

Mother Goose Set to Music, J. W. Elliott. McLaughlin & Co.

Seven Little Songs, Grant-Schaefer. Clayton F. Summy Co.

Fifty-five Rounds and Carols, Sara L. Dunning. G. Schirmer.

Folk Songs from Somerset, C. J. Sharp and C. L. Marson. Simpkin & Co., Schott & Co., London.

English Folk Songs for Schools, S. Baring Gould and C. J. Sharp. J. Curwen & Sons, Ltd., London.

Thirty-six Songs for Children, Grant-Schaefer. C. C. Birchard & Co., Boston.

Songs of Life and Nature, Eleanor Smith. Silver Burdett.

Songs for Little Children, Parts I-II, Eleanor Smith. Milton Bradley.

The Song Primer (Teachers' Book), Alys Bentley. A. S. Barnes.

Songs of the Child World, Riley and Gaynor. John Church Co.

Play Songs (from the Song Series), Alys E. Bentley. A. S. Barnes.

Songs of a Little Child's Day, Poulsson and Smith. Milton Bradley.

EDUCATION MUSIC COURSE, Teachers' Edition. Ginn.
SONG ECHOES FROM CHILD LAND, JENKS AND RUST. Oliver Ditson Co.
STEVENSON SONG BOOK. G. Schirmer.

SONGS FOR LITTLE CHIL-DREN

Part I

ELEANOR SMITH

A

Morning Prayer, 2.
The Morning Sun is Shining, 7.
All the Birds Have Come Again, 20.
Good-Bye to Summer, 22.
When the Snow is on the Ground, 28. (Mother Goose.)
The North Wind Doth Blow, 30. (Mother Goose.)
Little Boy Blue, 102.
Twinkle, Twinkle Little Star, 97.
Sleep, Baby, Sleep, 96.
I Love Little Pussy, 92. (Mother Goose.)
Rain Song, 88.
We are Little Soldier Men, 68.
Do the Little Brown Twigs Complain, 26.
The Autumn Leaves are Crying, 24.

Part II. B.

Harvest Song, 22.
The Chipmunks, 55.
Daffy-down-dilly, 82.
Flag Song, 112.

BENTLEY—THE SONG PRIMER

(Teachers' Book)

A

Santa Claus, 28.
The Golden-rod, 24.
Jack Frost, 38.
In a Hickory Nut, 34.
He Prayeth Best, 56.
Soldier Boys, 25.

Dancing Song, 33.
The Clock, 21.
The Rain, 18.
The Hurdy Gurdy, 19.
Cradle Song, 16.
The Echo, 24.
The Fiddle, 33.
The Wind, 35.
Dance of the Fairies, 40.
Day and Night, 43.
Nature's Good-night, 50.

MOTHER GOOSE SET TO MUSIC

ELLIOTT

A

The North Wind Doth Blow, 47.
The King of France, 37.
Hey, Diddle, Diddle, 50.
Nineteen Birds, 10.
Pussy-Cat, Pussy-Cat, 9.
Dickory, Dickory, Dock, 7.
Little Jack Horner, 22.
A, B, C, Tumble Down D, 25.
Sing a Song of Sixpence, 32.

SONGS OF THE CHILD WORLD

GAYNOR

A

Snow Flakes, 71.
Tracks in the Snow, 69.
The Leaves' Party, 64.
Farewell to the Bride. 66.
Jack Frost, 68.
The Sailor, 50.
Little Yellow Dandelion (Pussy Willow), 79
Robin Red-Breast, 73.

ROUNDS, CAROLS AND SONGS

Osgood

A

The Little Dreamer. Better in Bb, 5.

Schnick Schnack, 8.

There was a Little Woman. Better in Eb, 12.

Lightly Row, 14.

Fox and Goose, 15.

A, B, C, 16.

Pretty Birdlings, 6.

Kitty Cat and the Mouse, 16.

Come, Little Leaves, 18.

Hop, Hop, Hop! 19.

Sleep, Baby, Sleep! 20.

I've a Little Dog at Home, 24.

Fritz and Spitz, 30.

Lullaby, 37.

Morning Song, 43.

The Boy and the Wren, 45. Better in G.

Buy a Broom, 46.

Come, Lovely May, 47. Use translation in Bk. II. Eleanor Smith Course.

The Violet, 51.

Longing for Spring, 57.

Clip, Clap, 60.

Sleep, Darling, Sleep, 61. (A. II.) Key of F.

Hunter's Song, 62.

Winter, Good-bye, 63. Second Stanza better in Bk. II. E. S. Music Course.

Cold Winter is Round Us, 105. (A. II.)

The Shepherdess, 108.

Shall I Show You How the Farmer? 110. (A. II.)

The Fir and Pine, 111.

God Knows, 122.

Messenger of Spring, 42. (A. II.)

SMALL SONGS FOR SMALL SINGERS

Neidlinger

A

Snow-flakes, 29.

Mr. Duck and Mr. Turkey, 32.

Mr. Squirrel, 38.

Jack Frost, 46.

The Bluebird, 30.

Little Yellowhead, 53.

Mr. Frog, 28. Key of D preferable.

The Windy Day, 50.

The Caterpillar, 18.

The Tin Soldiers, 31. Key (D).

Tiddlely Winks, 19. Key (D).

The Bunny, 13.

The Chicken, 5.

The See-Saw, 10. (Eb.)

Falling Leaves, 12.

The Whale, 6.

The Robin's Song, 17.

The Wise Old Owl, 20.

Our Flag, 34.

Polly, 35.

The Kettle, 39.

The Spider, 40.

Little Birdie, 43.

Bubbles, 52.

Tick, Tock, 54.

SONGS AND GAMES FOR LITTLE ONES

Walker and Jenks

A

Grasshopper Green, 39, E.

Over the Bare Hills Far Away, 32, E.

The Bluebird, 29.

All the Birds Have Come Again, 27.

Canst Thou Count the Stars? 14.

Morning Hymn, 7. Key Bb.

Boat Song, 43.

Come, Little Leaves, Bb.
Where do all the Daisies Go? 47.
Winter Jewels, 54.
The Little New Year, 55, A.
The First Christmas, 60. Eb.
Shine Out, Oh Blessed Star, 63.
Good-Morning Song, 60.
Five Little Chickadees, 85.
My Pigeon-House, 86.

NATURE SONGS FOR CHIL-DREN

KNOWLTON

A

Snowballs, 63. Makes good game.
Patriotic Hymn, 102.
August, 18.
The Call of the Crow, 40.
Dandelion, 32.
The Dandelion, Cycle, 30.
Kite Time, 76.
The Postman, 56.
The Scissors Grinder, 60.
Feeding the Chickens, 59.

SONGS OF THE CHILD WORLD

GAYNOR

B

Christmas Carol, 29.
Sleighing Song, 70.
Harvest of Squirrel and Honey
Bee, 65.
Thanksgiving Song, 67.
The Tulips, 82.
Our Flag, 30.
Spinning the Yarn, 20.
Grandma's Knitting Song, 22.
The Black-Smith, 16.

SONGS OF LIFE AND NATURE

ELEANOR SMITH

B

Fairy Folk, 136. Stanzas 1 and 2.
Maypole Dance, 28.

SONG ECHOES FROM CHILD LAND

JENKS AND RUST

B

Santa Claus, 62.

SONGS FOR LITTLE CHIL-DREN

Part II

ELEANOR SMITH

B

Thanksgiving Song, 23.
Spin, Lassie, Spin, 16.

ART SONG CYCLES

MIESSNER

Bk. I.

B

Touching, 11.
Granddaddy Longlegs, 36.
In Germany, 41.

BENTLEY—THE SONG PRIMER

Teachers' Book

B

The Leaflets, 46.
The Shepherd Moon, 51. Eb.
A Pretty Passenger, 44.
Once I Got Into a Boat, 45.
The Train, 15.
The See-Saw, 20.
The Sea Shell, 17.
Wing Foo, 22.
The Butterfly, 26.

SEVEN LITTLE SONGS

GRANT-SCHAEFER

B

Spinning Song, 4.
Slumber Song, 12.

STEVENSON SONG BOOK

B

The Swing, 3.
The Wind, 59.
Windy Nights, 109.
Singing, 39.

MOTHER GOOSE SET TO MUSIC

ELLIOT

B

When the Snow is on the Ground, 42.
I Love Little Pussy, 51.
Ding, Dong, Bell, 8.
Jack and Jill, 2.
Little Bo-peep, 4.
Lullaby, 76.
Humpty Dumpty, 30.

EDUCATION MUSIC COURSE

Teachers' Edition

B

Where Do All the Daisies Go? 20.
Thanksgiving Day, 40. (Words difficult.)
May-Day Song, 47.
In Shadowtown, 144.
Fancies, 131.
The Flag We Love, 36.
A Christmas Song, 163.
The Passing Soldiers, 171.

NATURE SONGS FOR CHIL-DREN

KNOWLTON

B

January, 6.
Little Hickory Nut, 78.
What Robin Told, 38.

Rollicking Robin, 48. (Sing upper Bb each time.)
In the Tree-Top, 94.

ROUNDS, CAROLS AND SONGS

OSGOOD

B

Fiddle-De-Dee, 25.
Tooriletoo, 29.
Perrie, Merrie, Dixie, 34.
Golden   Slumbers,   52.   (c.) Change "wantons" to "darl-ings."
The Postilion, 56.
Hunter's Song, 62.
Holy Night, 67. (c.)
Child Jesus, 68.
Spinning Song, 85.
Sweet and Low, 96. (c.)
The Little Soldier, 102.
A Frog He Would a Wooing Go, 116.
The Shepherdess and the Cuckoo, 118.
Good King Wenceslas, 128. (c.)

SONGS FOR SCHOOLS

FARNSWORTH

B and C

America, 5.
National Hymn, 6.
Patriotic Hymn, 8.
America the Beautiful, 7.
The Red, White and Blue, 11.
Star-Spangled Banner, 12.
Dixie, 28.
Old Folks at Home, 22.

Old Kentucky Home, 25.
The Harp that Once, 56.
The Minstrel Boy, 40.
All Through the Night, 70.
Auld Lang Syne, 74.
Weel May the Keel Row, 66.
The Ash Grove, 50.
Forth to the Battle, 38.
The Hunt is Up, 44.
The Jolly Miller, 46.
Boola Song, 76.
Fair Harvard, 82.
Eton Boating Song, 84.
Sans Souci, 87.
Cornell Song, 98.
Wassail Song, 138.

SUPPLEMENT

Rule, Britannia.
Hymn of Thanks.
Silent Night.
Angel of Peace.
Now is the Month of Maying.
Under the Greenwood Tree.
Maypole Dance.
Tenting on the Old Camp Ground.
Old Black Joe.
The Waits.

ENGLISH FOLK SONGS FOR SCHOOLS

GOULD AND SHARP

B and C

The Wraggle, Taggle Gipsies, O!,
2.
The Fox, 64.
The Merry Haymakers, 54.
A Frog He Would a Wooing Go,
88.
The Frog and the Mouse, 90.
The Tailor and the Mouse, 100.
Sir John Barleycorn, 58.

FOLK SONGS FROM SOMER-SET

SHARP AND MARSON

B and C

Blow Away the Morning Dew, 16.
The Wraggle, Taggle Gipsies, O!,
18.
Lord Rendal, 46.
Brennan on the Moor, 52.

SONGS OF THE BRITISH ISLANDS

HADOW

B and C

Rule, Britannia, 92.
Under the Greenwood Tree, 66.
Now is the Month of Maying, 110.
Maypole Dance. (Come, Lassie
and Lad), 74.
Heart of Oak, 65.
The Spring is Coming, 60.
The Harp That Once, 43.
The Maypole, 78.
Drink to Me Only With Thine
Eyes, 52.
All Through the Night, 44.
The Keel Row, 25.
Golden Slumbers, 21.
The Jolly Miller, 16.
The Hunt is Up, 2.
God Save the King, 1.

THE CHILDREN'S MESSIAH

HOFER

B and C

Carol, Brothers, Carol, 4.
Christmas Day in the Morning, 7.
Christmas Eve, 16.

Three Kings of Orient. 26.
What Child is This? 28.
O, Holy Night, 30.
Silent Night, 33.

SONGS OF LIFE AND NATURE

ELEANOR SMITH

C

Pussy Willow's Secret, 16.
Snowwhite, 138.
Ring Out, Wild Bells, 11.

The Fir-Tree, 164.
King Richard, Lion-heart, 87.
Harvest Song, 35.

SONG YEAR BOOK

HELEN PLACE

C

September, 9.
October, 19.
The Fir-Tree, 28.
Christmas Eve, 38.
Sunlight in Winter, 58.

ENGLISH

The study of English naturally occupies an important place in the school program. Regarding it as the most efficient means of culture at our command, we make it the "core," as Dr. Nicholas Murray Butler styles it, of our curriculum, devoting more time to it than to any other subject, and considering it the chief standard for measuring the progress and ability of our pupils.

Our aim is the obvious one—to train the children to use their mother-tongue more effectively in speaking and writing, and to gain some knowledge and appreciation of its literature. In school-room practice the subject groups itself as follows:

1. Reading and Literature
2. Composition
3. Language Work and Grammar
4. Spelling

READING AND. LITERATURE

The first division, READING AND LITERATURE, includes the work incident to the mechanical mastery of the printed page, practice in the art of oral reading, and the study of such selections from literature as have been judged appropriate to the various grades.

The details of the work involved in gaining the mechanical mastery of the printed page referred to above are too well known to need explanation here. The books that have been found best suited to the purpose are mentioned in the outline that follows.

The second phase of the work in Reading and Literature which, for want of a better title, is called practice in the art of oral reading, is directed towards bringing about a free, simple, natural style of reading with clear, distinct enunciation and well-modulated, agreeable tones. For this practice reading books which are graded a year below the designated grade are used. This arrangement places in the child's hands a text that offers few technical difficulties and thus enables him to give his undivided attention to the problem of oral expression.

The third phase of work in the course in Reading and Literature consists of the study of the masterpieces of English prose and verse that have been selected for the year. In the lower grades, where the children can do little reading themselves, the work is done principally by means of stories told by the teacher. As the child's ability to read grows, these stories naturally diminish in number, but this type of work is found so valuable that it is made use of even in the upper grammar grades. How varied the stories are in scope and character may be gathered from the outlines that follow. These lists are, of course, suggestive rather than fixed. Each teacher varies her stories from year to year, being guided in her selection by the particular needs of her class, or by some specific purpose that she may have in mind.

The literature that is placed in the children's hands is selected on much the same principle; the needs and interests of the child, his ability, other subject matter of the grade, and the plans and purposes of the school in general, all enter as factors. As great a variety as is consistent with the controlling motives is introduced. The treatment naturally varies with the character of the selection and with the motive of its introduction. Long stories, such as " Ivanhoe " and " Dombey and Son," are read rapidly for their plot and their pictures of the times, other shorter selections such as " Rip Van Winkle," " The Legend of Sleepy Hollow," and Lowell's " Yussouf," for careful character study, still others primarily for their humor, while others, especially poems, are studied for their music, their pictures, and their power to inspire.

Certain favorite selections are memorized in each grade. This list, too, varies with the class, with individual preferences, and with the teacher's purpose. Each grade, however, holds itself responsible for committing to memory a number of the finest selections on its list. These are reviewed from year to year and new ones are added that the children may have gradually stored in their minds some of the treasures that are their English birthright.

COMPOSITION

The second of the groups into which the English work of the school naturally divides itself is COMPOSITION. The term as here used is a broad one, embracing oral and written reproductions in the form of riddles, jokes, anecdotes, stories, descriptions, topical recitations in history, geography, nature-study and other subjects of the grade as well as original oral and written work along lines that appeal to the interests of the child, simple dramatization, and the writing of occasional verse. Acting on the principle that children learn their mother-tongue by imitation, the best models possible are placed before them both for conscious and unconscious imitation. In the lower grades the models are usually stories told by the teacher. This does not mean that all of the teacher's stories are reproduced; only the shorter, simpler ones are used for this purpose. These are found most effective models, the child reproducing unconsciously the vocabulary, the expression, even the enunciation that he has heard. In the higher grades the style of an author is frequently studied and deliberately imitated by the pupils either orally or in writing. This does not imply a slavish imitation, one that curbs the child's spontaneity and encourages him to express himself in an unnatural, stilted style. It means rather a study of the idea embodied in the model and of the author's skill in presenting this idea, and next the application of the author's methods to some experience of the child's own. For instance, in describing his first fishing excursion, Whittier dilates upon the pleasure he experienced when he received his first fishing-rod, next he dwells upon the delights of the walk over field and meadow to the trout-brook, then he describes his sensations at the catching of the first big fish and at its loss as it slipped from the hook at the moment of landing, and finally he pictures his effort to overcome his disappointment and to persevere until he met with success.

In using this story as a model for imitation, the children may describe their first skating experience, or their first attempt at swimming, or at horse-back riding, following the general plan of the model, that is, dividing their story into scenes corresponding in character to those of the story imitated. They may also adopt the author's scheme of beginning with a sentence that provokes interest, his method of leading up to a climax, and even such of his words and phrases as please them.

In the first three years most of the composition is oral. In addition to the retelling of stories, the children are encouraged to talk freely about the things in and out of school that interest them. They bring their pets to the class room, birds, rabbits, gold-fish, turtles, and tell their classmates how they care for the little creatures, and describe their habits and cunning tricks. They bring unusual toys and explain their mechanism, they tell of visits to the farm, the park, the museum, and to other places of interest. The object of the work is primarily to develop the child's power of expression, but it also gives opportunity for some training in orderly arrangement and sequence.

In the upper grades oral reproductions in the form of stories, anecdotes, and topical recitations in the various subjects of the grade play an important part. Here, too, free expression is encouraged; current topics are discussed, questions pertaining to individual, class, school, or civic honor and loyalty are talked over, debates are held, and individual experiences are related.

Written work is begun toward the close of the first year. In this grade and in the second the written composition is usually class or coöperative work, as only by this method can bad habits of spelling and punctuation be avoided. (As an example of this kind of work see the lesson on "A Riddle" under the Composition Outline for the second grade.) Even in the third grade little individual written-work of an original character is expected, and that only after such careful oral preparation that there is no excuse for technical errors.

In order that written composition may not be a bugbear, topics are chosen in which the children are interested and about which they have an abundance to say; and sufficient preparation is made orally to give them confidence in their power to express themselves effectively. On the other hand topics are avoided on which there is so much to say that a long theme is necessary. In fact, the subjects assigned are generally so limited in scope that they demand very brief treatment. Throughout the school short and frequent written exercises are the rule.

Even in the upper grammar grades it is seldom that a theme more than a page in length is required. This, of course, debars such topics as " Joan of Arc," or " My Summer in Camp " and substitutes something more restricted as " Joan of Arc's Childhood," " Joan's Visions," "A Rainy Day in Camp," or "An Exciting Camp Experience."

By thus limiting the length of the theme, we rob composition work of its most dreaded feature, its mechanical laboriousness. Given an interesting topic on which he feels himself competent to write, and one that does not necessitate a tiresome amount of mechanical effort, the child goes at his task with confidence and pleasure.

LANGUAGE AND GRAMMAR

The third group of subjects under the general head of English includes technical work in language and such facts and principles of grammar as contribute to the work in literature and composition. As a matter of economy the ordinary rules of capitalization and punctuation are taught in the lower grades, while the work in formal grammar is left for the last two years of the elementary course, the sixth and seventh. This work is so systematized that each grade holds itself responsible for certain technical points in language as definitely as it holds itself responsible for prescribed arithmetical facts.

SPELLING

Much thought and attention has been given of late to the subject of spelling. Tests made in the various grades seem to prove without a doubt that better results are obtained when the lesson is taught in school than when the child studies it at home. These tests also established the fact that there is great economy of time in the former method. By means of the close concentration that the teacher demands as much is accomplished in ten minutes of class-study as the child, left to his own devices, accomplishes in double that time.

As a result of this investigation, spelling throughout the grades is taught in the class room, the period being given in part to the teaching of the lesson, and in part to the testing of the work. The number of new words taught in each lesson is not over three in the Third and Fourth grades, and not over four in the Fifth, Sixth, and Seventh, and often, when the words are difficult, the number is still smaller.

The words to be taught are selected with great care. Class lists are compiled from such sources as " The Spelling Vocabularies of Personal and Business Letters " by Leonard P. Ayres of the Russell Sage Foundation, and from the children's own vocabularies.

The experiments referred to above are described in full in Teachers College Record for January, 1912. A brief statement of the method of teaching spelling in vogue in the school follows.

Steps in Teaching Spelling

1. Write one of the words on the blackboard and teach it in accordance with the following plan. Then write the next word, teaching it in the same way. Continue in this way throughout the list.

    (a) While writing the word, *pronounce* it distinctly.

    (b) Develop the *meaning* orally either by calling for a sentence using the word or by giving its definition.

    (c) Divide word into syllables. Call on pupils to spell orally by syllables. Have them indicate what part of the word presents difficulties, or whether the word contains parts they already know.

    (d) Have pupils write the word, pronouncing it softly as they write.

    (e) Allow the class a moment in which to look at the word again, and then have them close their eyes and try to visualize it, or use any other device of a similar nature. Have considerable repetition, both oral and written.

2. After the various words of the day's lesson have been studied in this way, allow a few moments for studying again the whole list, suggesting that each pupil emphasize the words he thinks most difficult. This time should be limited so that every pupil will attend vigorously and intensively. Call upon pupils individually and in concert to spell the whole list without looking at the board. Refer them to the board again when they hesitate.

3. Erase all words from the blackboard and dictate to the class, using each word in a sentence first, then pronouncing it distinctly alone.

OUTLINE OF WORK IN READING AND LITERATURE
GRADE I
Reading Material

The Riverside Primer	} Van Sickle and Seegmiller Houghton Mifflin
Child Classics Primer	Alexander
Child Classics First Reader	Bobbs Merrill
Rhyme and Story Primer	McMahon—D. C. Heath
First Reader	} S u m m e r s—Frank D. Beathes Co.
First Reader	} Free and Treadwell— Rowe, Stevenson & Co.

Poems Studied

The Cow	
¹Bed in Summer	
¹Windy Nights	
My Shadow	
The Little Land	Stevenson
¹The Land of Story Book	
The Lamplighter	
¹The Swing	
The Snow-Bird	
Song for Winter	
Hide and Seek	Little Folk Lyrics
Snowflakes	Frank Dempster Sherman
The Fairies' Dream	
March	
¹April	
Wild Geese	
¹Little Gustava	Celia Thaxter
Chanticleer	
¹The Wind	Christina Rosetti
¹The Throstle	Tennyson
Putting the World to **Bed**	
Baby Ferns	Nature Study
Little Snowflakes	Charles Scott
A·Laughing Chorus	Nature in Verse
The First Snow-Drop	Lovejoy

¹ Memorized.

Stories Told by the Teacher

²Cinderella	Grimm
²Sleeping Beauty	Grimm
The Discontented Pine Tree	Andersen
The Ugly Duckling	Andersen
²The Three Pigs	Green Fairy Book
The Three Bears	Lang
²The Half Chick	
Little Red Riding Hood	Blue Fairy Book Lang
The Dove and the Ant	
The Boy and the Wolf	
The Dog and his Shadow	Æsop
²The Sun and the Wind	
The Lion and the Mouse	
²The Elves and the Shoemaker	
²The Gingerbread Man	Stories to Tell Children
²The Hen and the Grain of Wheat	Sara Cone Bryant
Another Little Red Hen	
²The Pied Piper of Hamelin	How to Tell Stories to
²Why the Trees Keep Their Leaves all Winter	Children Sara Cone Bryant
The Old Woman and Her Pig	
The Wheat Field	Laura Richards
²Pig Brother	
²The North Wind	The Child's World
Santa Claus and the Mouse	Poulsson
The Christ Child	
Picciola	Story Hour Kate Douglas Wiggin
Prince Harweda	Story Hour Harrison
The Musicians of Bremen	Grimm
Raggylug	Ernest Thompson-Seton
Chicken Little	Child Life—Second Reader Blaisdell
Three Little Goats Gruff	Graded Literature Readers —First Book

² Stories dramatized or retold by the children.

GRADE II

Reading Material

Riverside First Reader	Van Sickle and Seegmiller
The Progressive Road to Reading	Burchill, Ettinger, and Shimer
Second Reader	Hervey and Hix
Merry Animal Tales	Bigham
Second Reader	Free and Treadwell
Second Reader	Baker and Carpenter
Children's Classics in Dramatic Form—Book II	} Augusta Stevenson
Hiawatha (selections)	Longfellow
Mewanee, the Little Indian Boy	Belle Wiley
Child Lore	Bryce

Poems Studied

[3]A Day	Emily Dickinson
[3]The Cloud (extracts)	Shelley
[3]The Night Wind	Eugene Field
[3]The Gingham Dog	Eugene Field
[3]The Owl	Tennyson
[3]The Elf's Umbrella	O. Herford
[3]One, Two, Three	H. C. Bunner
Seven Times One	Jean Ingelow
Lullaby of the Iroquois	Pauline Johnson
Indian Cradle Song	
Indian Mother's Lullaby	Chas. Myall
[3]The Rainbow	
[3]The Firefly	
[3]The Moon	} Hiawatha Longfellow
[3]The Owls	
[3]Sleep Song	
The Swallows (selections)	Edwin Arnold
Four Winds	E. C. Stedman
An Open Secret	Unknown
Nonsense Alphabet	Edward Lear

---

[3] Memorized.

Goop Rhymes	Gelett Burgess
The Shepherd	Blake
Verses for Children (selections)	E. V. Lucas
Up, up, ye Dames	Coleridge
Sing Song (selections)	Christina Rosetti
Child's Garden of Verse (selections)	Stevenson
Little-Folk Lyrics (selections)	Sherman
Child Lyrics (selections)	J. Tabb

Stories Told or Read by the Teacher

⁴Phaeton—sun god	
⁴Mercury—wind god	
⁴Endymion—shepherd	Stories of Old Greece
⁴Latona—the frog	Firth
Baucis and Philemon	
David and Goliath	
Twenty-third Psalm	Bible
Christmas Story	
⁴The Fire Bringer	
⁴The Story of Little Tavwots	
The Cat and the Parrot	
Hans in Luck	Stories to tell to Children
⁴Epaminondas and his Auntie	How to tell Stories to
⁴How Brother Rabbit fooled the Whale and Mr. Elephant	Children
	Best Stories to tell to Children
⁴The Little Jackal and the Alligator	Sara Cone Bryant
Billy Beg and his Bull	
Rumpelstiltskin	
Legend of Saint Christopher	Schonberg Cotta Family (adapted)
The Legend of Arbutus	The Children's Hour
Saint George and the Dragon	Bailey and Lewis
Hiawatha (selections)	Longfellow
Robinson Crusoe (selections)	Defoe

⁴ Stories dramatized or retold by the children.

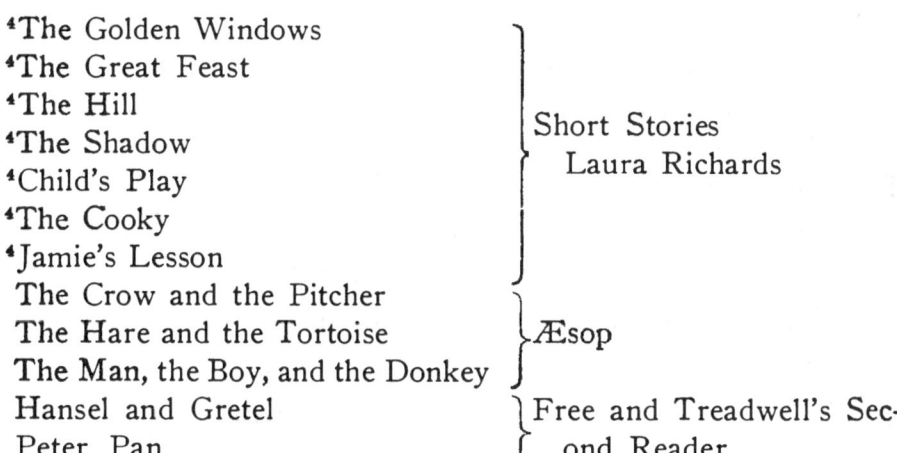

⁴The Golden Windows ⎫
⁴The Great Feast ⎪
⁴The Hill ⎪
⁴The Shadow ⎬ Short Stories
⁴Child's Play ⎪   Laura Richards
⁴The Cooky ⎪
⁴Jamie's Lesson ⎭

The Crow and the Pitcher ⎫
The Hare and the Tortoise ⎬ Æsop
The Man, the Boy, and the Donkey ⎭

Hansel and Gretel ⎫ Free and Treadwell's Sec-
Peter Pan ⎭   ond Reader

GRADE III

Reading Material

Riverside Second Reader	Van Sickle and Seegmiller
Third Reader	Hervey and Hix
Aldine Third Reader	Spaulding and Bryce
Pinocchio	Collodi
Alice in Wonderland	Lewis Carroll
Art Literature Reader—Book III	Frances E. Chutter
In the Days of Giants	⎫ Abbey Farwell Brown
Book of Saints and Friendly Beasts	⎭

Poems Studied

⁵Psalm XXIII	Bible
⁵October's Bright Blue Weather	H. H. Jackson
⁵Clouds	⎫ Little Folk Lyrics
Wizard Frost	⎬ Frank Dempster Sherman
A Real Santa Claus	⎭
⁵The Children's Hour	Longfellow
Fairy Folk	⎫ Allingham (U. P.*)
⁵Wishing	⎭
A Sudden Shower	⎫ James Whitcomb Riley
Little Orphant Annie	⎭
⁵Seein' Things at Night	Eugene Field
Suppose	Alice Cary

---
⁴ Stories dramatized or retold by the children.
⁵ Memorized.

⁵How the Leaves Came Down	S. Coolidge (U. P.*)
⁵The Night Before Christmas	Moore (U. P.)
A Wonderful Weaver	Anonymous (U. P.)
Laughing Chorus	Anonymous (U. P.)
The Wonderful World	Wm. B. Rands (U. P.)
Guessing Chorus	Johnstone (U. P.)

Stories Told or Read by the Teacher

⁶The Story of Joseph	Bible
⁶Arachne	⎫ Mythland
Prometheus	⎬ Beckwith
Ares	⎭
Little Claus and Big Claus	Andersen
⁶Snow-White and the Seven Dwarfs	Grimm
⁶The Stag	⎫ Stories to tell Children
The Fir Tree	⎪ How to tell Stories to
The Golden Cobweb	⎪ Children
⁶The Hero of Haarlem	⎭ Sara Cone Bryant
⁶The Endless Tale	⎫ Fifty Famous Stories
⁶The Wise Men of Gotham	⎬ Baldwin
King Alfred Stories	⎭
Rikki-Tiki-Tavi	⎱ Jungle Book ⎰ Kipling
Lobo	Ernest Thompson-Seton
The Bear Story	James Whitcomb Riley
Uncle Remus (selections)	Joel Chandler Harris
Hiawatha (selections)	Longfellow
The Town Mouse and the Country Mouse	Æsop

GRADE IV

Selections Read and Studied

Riverside Third Reader	Van Sickle and Seegmiller
Child Classics, Third Reader	Alexander
Water Babies	Kingsley

* U. P.—Unit Poems, published by the Unit Press, Fitchburg, Massachusetts, are printed upon loose leaflets of uniform size.

⁵Memorized.

⁶ Stories dramatized or retold by children.

King of the Golden River	Ruskin
Birds of Killingworth	⎫
The Bell of Atri	⎬ Longfellow
The Village Blacksmith	⎭
⁷Psalm C	⎫ Bible
⁷St. Luke II, 8-14	⎭
⁷He Prayeth well	Coleridge
⁷Out of the Morning	Dickinson
⁷The Sandpiper	Celia Thaxter
September	H. H. Jackson
The Daffodils	Wordsworth
The Desert	W. W. Story
⁷The River Song	Water Babies, Kingsley
⁷Dutch Lullaby	⎫ Field
⁷Norse Lullaby	⎭
⁷America	Samuel Smith
The Camel's Hump (poem)	Kipling
A Boy's Song	Hogg

In addition to the above each child memorizes two or three poems of his own choosing—subject to the teacher's approval.

Stories Told or Read by the Teacher

Daniel in the Lion's Den	Bible
Horatius	Macaulay
The Wanderings of Ulysses (selections)	Lamb
Damon and Pythias	⎱ Ethics for Children ⎰ Ella Lyman Cabot
The Gulf in the Forum	Livy. Adapted
Quiquern	⎱ Jungle Book
White Seal	⎰ Kipling
Uncle Remus (selections)	Joel Chandler Harris
The King of the Birds	⎫
Faithful John	⎬ Grimm
The Seven Ravens	⎭
The Brave Tin Soldier	⎱ Andersen
What the Goodman does is Right	⎰

⁷ Memorized.

The Crab and his Mother	Æsop
Bruce and the Spider	Scott
The Patient Cat	Laura E. Richards
Why the Ears of Wheat are Small	} Language Through Nature and Art — Perdue and Griswold

GRADE V

Selections Read and Studied

Riverside Fourth Reader	Van Sickle and Seegmiller
Wonder Book	Hawthorne
Tanglewood Tales	Hawthorne
Heide	Spyri
[8]Psalm XXIV	Bible
While Shepherds Watched their Flocks by Night	Nahum Tate
[8]Abou Ben Adhem	Leigh Hunt
[8]Heaven is not reached at a Single Bound	J. G. Holland
[8]Down to Sleep	H. H. Jackson
The Brook	Tennyson
The Planting of the Apple Tree	Bryant
[8]The Voice of Spring	Felicia Hemans
The Boys and the Apple Tree	Taylor
The Song Sparrow	Van Dyke
The Farm-Yard Song	Trowbridge
The Mountain and the Squirrel	Emerson
The Blind Men and the Elephant	Saxe
Contentment	Holmes
The Wreck of the Hesperus	Longfellow
[8]Charge of the Light Brigade	Tennyson
The Legend of Bishop Hatto	} Southey
*The Inchcape Rock	
Snowbound (selections)	Whittier
The Overland Mail	Kipling

* Memorized.

Note.—Most of the poems, unless otherwise noted, are taken from "Poems Every Child Should Know," by Mary E. Burt.

Stories Read or Told by the Teacher

David and Goliath	
David and Jonathan	} Bible
David and Saul	
King Arthur Stories (selections)	Howard Pyle
The Story of Roland	} Fifth Reader Baker and Carpenter
The Wonderful Adventures of Nils (selections)	Selma Lagerlof
The Birds' Christmas Carol (selections)	Wiggin
Aladdin and the Wonderful Lamp	Arabian Nights
The Cat that Walked by Himself	} Just So Stories Kipling
William Tell	} Child Classics, Fourth Reader—Knowles
Moni, the Goat Boy	} Spyri
The Little Runaway	
The Finest Lesson of the Year	De Amicis
The Mouse and the Moonbeam	Field

GRADE VI

Selections Read and Studied

Riverside Fifth Reader	Van Sickle and Seegmiller
Ivanhoe	Scott
Rip Van Winkle	} Irving
Legend of Sleepy Hollow	
Courtship of Miles Standish	
Evangeline (selections)	
King Robert of Sicily	} Longfellow
The Skeleton in Armor	
Paul Revere's Ride	
How they Brought the Good News from Ghent to Aix	
Incident of the French Camp	} Browning
Herve Riel	

⁹Sweet and **Low**
⁹The Eagle   } Tennyson
The Revenge
⁹Ring out Wild Bells

Yussouf   Lowell
⁹Landing of the Pilgrim Fathers   Hemans
⁹Old Ironsides   Holmes
⁹Patriotism   Scott
Columbus   Joaquin Miller
⁹O Captain! My Captain!   Walt Whitman
The Burial of Moses   Cecil F. Alexander
Sir Patrick Spens   Old Ballad
⁹A Sea Song   Allan Cunningham
⁹The Sea   Barry Cornwall
Battle of Blenheim   Southey
⁹Psalm XIX   Bible

Stories Read or Told by the Teacher

The Story of Ruth   } Bible
Stories of Moses

The Three Questions   } Twenty-Three Tales
                                  Tolstoi

The Three Boxes   } Stories from the Rabbis
                                  A. S. Isaacs

The Great Stone Face   Hawthorne
The Marvelous Tower   Irving
Sir Galahad   Tennyson
Sinbad the Sailor   Arabian Nights

The Griffin and the Minor Canon } Fanciful Tales
                                     Stockton

The Merry Adventures of Robin
    Hood (selections)   Howard Pyle

The Ship that Found Herself   } The Day's Work
                                  Kipling

---

⁹ Memorized.

GRADE VII

Selections Read and Studied

School Speaker and Reader	Hyde
Paul Dombey—Selections from Dombey and Son	⎫
A Christmas Carol	⎬ Dickens ⎭
A-hunting of the Deer	Warner
Birds and Bees	⎫ Burroughs
Pepacton	⎭
[10]Lincoln's Gettysburg Speech	
[10]Speech of Patrick Henry in the Virginia Convention	
[10]Civic Creed	McDowell
[10]Psalm CXXI	Bible
[10]Concord Hymn	Emerson
Warren's Address	Pierpont
[10]The Recessional	⎫
Ballad of East and West	⎬ Kipling
Fuzzy Wuzzy	⎭
The Destruction of Sennacherib	Byron
[10]The Spacious Firmament on High	Addison
[10]A Vagabond Song	Bliss Carman
The Lady of Shalott	Tennyson
The Forsaken Merman	Matthew Arnold
The Vision of Sir Launfal	Lowell
[10]The Snow Storm	Emerson
Selections from Burns	

Stories Read or Told by the Teacher

The Story of Elijah	Bible
The Perfect Tribute	Mary Shipman Andrews
Autobiography of John Muir	
Stickeen	John Muir
A Message to Garcia	Elbert Hubbard
Story of a Salmon	David Starr Jordan
Story of Jean Valjean	Victor Hugo

[10] Memorized.

OUTLINE OF WORK IN COMPOSITION

GRADE I

Oral.   (Almost all of the work is oral.)

1. Reproduction.   Stories told in school and at home.

   The teacher's stories which are used for reproduction will be found marked 1 in the *Outline of Work in Reading and Literature,* Grade I.

2. Original.

   Descriptions of pets, toys, etc.

   Accounts of trips and holiday experiences.

   Dramatization of simple stories.

Written.

1. A letter.

   This is the first written work of the year.   A sample letter with the method employed in teaching is given below.

2. Simple statements.   Towards the close of the year one or more stories are reduced to a few essential statements and are reproduced from memory.

(Letter)

Dear Mother,

I love you.

Mary.

This letter is written on the black-board by the teacher and the pupils are told that as soon as they can write it without a copy, they may post it.

Method.

The word *Mother* is written on the board in a large, free hand. The children trace the word in the air with the same free arm movement.   The word is erased.   Several children go to the board and try to write it from memory.   Letters that give trouble are worked on individually until the word can be easily written. Each word is taken up in a similar manner.   When a child can write the whole letter on the board—

Dear Mother,

I love you.

and sign his name, he is given paper on which to write it. Much attention is given to good writing position and to freedom of movement.

GRADE II

Oral. (The work is largely oral.)
1. Reproduction.
Stories told in school and at home.
The teacher's stories which are used for reproduction will be found marked 4 in the *Outline of Work in Reading and Literature,* Grade II.
2. Original.
Descriptions.
Simple experiments in physics.
Excursions to garden, etc.
How to play a game.
How to make things.
How to go from school to home.
Rhyming games—(Dumb Crambo).

Written.
1. Original Riddles.
A sample riddle with the method employed in teaching is given below.
2. Original class rhymes.
3. Descriptions of the season—weather.
4. Stories of imagination: If Jack-o-lantern should come to life, what would he say? (Two or three sentences.)
5. Stories suggested by pictures.

A Riddle

One child is sent out of the room. Those remaining decide to make a riddle about the cat. One child suggests, *I can climb a tree;* another, *I see in the dark.* When the sentences meet with class approval they are written on the board by the teacher. The riddle may then read—

I can climb a tree. I see in the dark.
I can purr and mew. I do not like dogs.
What am I?

The child who was sent out of the room is now recalled to guess the riddle. The paragraph is then studied for capitalization, spelling, punctuation. Finally the riddle is written from memory, or if it is too long for a pure memory exercise it may be written from a copy on the board from which the specially studied words have been erased.

GRADE III

Oral.

1. Reproduction.

Stories told in school and at home.

The teacher's stories which are used for reproduction will be found marked 5 in the *Outline of Work in Reading and Literature,* Grade III.

2. Original.

Stories of personal experience.

Descriptions of simple experiments, of excursions, of work done in manual training and nature-study.

(In all story telling a special point is made of arrangement, telling the story in *scenes,* to develop paragraph idea.)

Written.

Oral work still predominates in this grade. Careful preparation is made for all written work by means of class discussion and by the writing of difficult words on the blackboard.

1. Reproduction.
2. Short poems written from memory.
3. Original class stories.
4. Original poems.
5. Letters. Children are given heading and closing.
6. Description of trips and of other lines of work.

GRADE IV

From the fourth grade on, oral composition is not distinguished from written in the outline.

Reproduction.

Different ways of expressing a thought.

Poems and short prose selections written from memory.

Letters—friendly.

Stories suggested by pictures.

Original fables in imitation of model.

Original stories.

Original poems.

Dialogues.

Dramatizations.

GRADE V

Reproduction.

Different ways of expressing a thought.

Poems and short prose selections written from memory.

Letters—the friendly letter—the social note.

Practice in changing from one sentence form to another.

Stories, fables, descriptions in imitation of model.

Stories suggested by pictures.

Original endings for stories.

Dialogues.

Dramatizations.

Reports of excursions and lectures.

Original stories and accounts of personal experiences.

Original poems.

GRADE VI

Reproduction.

Different ways of expressing a thought.

Poems and short prose selections written from memory.

Letters—social notes—friendly letters—business letters.

Stories in imitation of model.

Stories suggested by pictures.

Original beginnings—original endings for stories.

Dialogues.

Dramatizations.

Character sketches.

Explanation of processes—definite directions for doing things and for finding places.

Reports of lectures and excursions.

Original stories and accounts of personal experiences.

Application of proverbs.

Description of picture suggested by lines of poetry or prose.
Descriptions of persons and places.
Original poems.

GRADE VII

Reproduction.
Different ways of expressing a thought.
Poems and short prose selections written from memory.
Letters—friendly and business letters.
Dialogues.
Dramatizations.
Stories in imitation of model.
Explanation of processes.
Reports of lectures, excursions, etc.
Expanding sentences into paragraphs.
Condensing paragraphs.
Book reviews.
Descriptions of persons and places.
Original stories and accounts of personal experiences.
Original poems.
The oral composition frequently consists of one- or two-minute
speeches on current topics or on personal experiences.

OUTLINE OF WORK IN LANGUAGE AND GRAMMAR
GRADE I

Capital letter at beginning of sentence.
Period at end of sentence.
Child's own name.
Pronoun *I*.
GRADE II
Child's own address—capitals and punctuation marks involved.
Abbreviations Mr., Mrs., Dr., and names of months.
Capital in days of week, months, holidays.
Dates.
Capital at beginning of each line of poetry.
Interrogation point.

GRADE III

Exclamation point.

Contractions as *don't, won't, I'm, I'll,* etc.

Abbreviations as needed.

Capitals in names of places.

Indentation of paragraphs—paragraph idea developed.

Friendly letter form, including addressing of envelope, introduced. Children are not held responsible for heading and close of letter. These are written on board by teacher and copied by class whenever a letter is written.

Homonyms,

to	too	two	here	hear
their	there		our	hour

GRADE IV

Apostrophe in the singular possessive case.

The undivided quotation.

Comma in a series.

Titles of books, poems, etc.

Friendly letter form—addressing envelope emphasized.

Stricter attention to form and margins.

Paragraph idea continued—writing from outlines.

Use of dictionary introduced.

Alphabetical arrangement of lists of words beginning with different letters; beginning with the same letter.

Common homonyms.

GRADE V

Apostrophe in singular and plural possessive.

Divided and undivided quotations.

Comma—in series, in address, after *yes* and *no.*

Capitalization of words derived from names of peoples and places.

Letter form; formal and informal social notes.

Paragraphs—the three-paragraph form in composition: the beginning, the middle, the closing.

Use of dictionary—simplest diacritical marks.

Kinds of sentences.

Declarative, Interrogative,
Imperative, Exclamatory.

GRADE VI

Business letter forms.

Paragraph. Logical arrangement of sentences in paragraph; the three-paragraph form continued, namely beginning, middle, closing.

Use of dictionary for spelling, for meaning, for pronunciation.

Subject and predicate, complete and simple.

Phrase, adjective and adverbial.

Recognition of the parts of speech.

GRADE VII

Comma—in phrase, in compound sentence.

Paragraph—Topic sentence.

Complements—subjective, direct object.

Verbs—transitive, intransitive, copulative.

Modifiers—words, phrases, clauses.

Compound sentences.

Complex sentences.

PENMANSHIP

The aim of the formal drill lessons in penmanship is to produce speed as well as a reasonable degree of legibility in handwriting. In Grades One and Two more emphasis is placed upon the correct form of letters than upon movement exercises, while in the grades that follow about equal emphasis is placed upon form and speed. The standard of letter forms and slant is set by The New Barnes Writing Books by C. S. and A. G. Hammock. The use of these copy-books in regular class drill is left to the option of the individual teacher.

Special classes in penmanship are formed for all pupils of Grades Six and Seven whose handwriting does not conform to Quality 12 of the Thorndike Scale. As soon as the penmanship of a pupil does measure up to the class standard, he is excused from this special drill class.

NATURE-STUDY

Nature-study appears upon the official program as occurring two or three times a week for the first five years of the elementary school,—the periods occupying twenty minutes in the first three grades and a half-hour in the fourth and fifth grades. But as the work is often out-doors, in the garden or campus or parks, we take advantage of fair weather and go forth as opportunity offers; or if the children are tired from other work, they go to the garden to dig or to plant or just to see "what is happening." Again some of our best work is done before school or during recess or in a five-minute impromptu lesson on some specimen brought in by an eager child who wants to know more about it.

In regard to subject matter, whatever belongs to the natural environment of the normal child is legitimate material. Every individual is the center of his own universe, and the naturally widening circles of his environment furnish new material from year to year. Our subject matter includes the animals and plants that are the sources of our everyday food, clothing, and shelter; animals and plants that are beneficial or injurious in the production of these sources; animals that make good pets; plants that make beautiful our windows, gardens, and parks; and such wild flowers as are within reach of the children.

Our resources for material are greater than our city environment suggests at first sight. To begin with, we have our window-gardens and such aquaria and vivaria as it seems wise to keep in our school-rooms, and a school-garden which, though too small to allow much individual work, is yet of priceless value in that it gives the children sufficient practical experience in gardening to enable them to make gardens of their own during the long summer vacation if they have any possible opportunity. Also we have a small greenhouse where we grow plants in winter and where we keep some of our larger pets.

There are still a few vacant lots within easy reach, and we make the most of the Lower Campus of Columbia University which is just across the street. Riverside and Morningside parks are available and also the Rambles in Central Park which is our favorite place for bird-study. Afternoon outings and excursions to the Palisades across the Hudson or to Van Cortlandt Park and vicinity are frequent, and the work in the Fourth and Fifth grades is supplemented by trips to the American Museum of Natural History, and to the Botanical and Zoological Gardens in the Bronx.

Almost without exception the children of the Horace Mann School spend their summers out of the city, but they do not return to us in the fall with any uniformity of experience. In order then to give our first grade children a common experience, we take them to a farm for a day. This is followed by a visit to a city market, so that they may realize that back of the market is the farm and garden. They lay out a miniature farm in the sand-pile, and begin gardening by gathering seeds to plant in the spring.

In October, each first grade child plants a hyacinth bulb in a pot and puts it away in the cold and dark until it is time to bring it out to blossom for Easter, when it is taken home to mother. They watch the earth getting ready for winter; they bring in caterpillars from the garden and watch them make cocoons; they see a squirrel's nest in the park and watch the squirrel to find out how he gets ready for winter. In the spring they plant the seeds that they saved, watch the growth and flowering of their hyacinths, and see a moth or butterfly come out of a cocoon. Wherever it is possible to carry over a line of work from fall to spring it is done to the end that the children may see that nature-study is a continued story and not just a picture-book.

In the winter when the supply of material is lowest, the visiting rabbit comes and spends a week or more in a big cage in the school-room. By watching him the children try to find out all the things that a rabbit can do. They learn how a rabbit takes care of himself, what his natural home is like, what he eats and where he gets his food, how he spends the winter and what keeps him warm, how he keeps himself clean, who his enemies are and how he protects himself from them. They decide that the rabbit makes a good pet because he is clean and pretty and sometimes playful, and because he is contented and happy. Finally they consider what they themselves can do to make him more contented and happy. Except for aquaria and small vivaria we consider the visiting pet more desirable and hygienic in the school-room than the permanent one.

The spring garden work of the First Grade is carried over into the Second Grade in the fall and the children gather their flowers for the school-room, to take home to mother or to send to some sick child. In order to have flowers to send to sick children in the spring, they plant a bed of bulbs in the garden in the fall. They add to their knowledge of the first year the names of more flowers, trees and birds, choosing those that naturally fall within the widening circle of interest and environment. They become interested in a new line of work,— simple experiments or problems involving the collection of considerable material: they find out how a plant gets out of a seed by planting seeds between glass and blotting-paper; they learn why sunlight is necessary by putting seedlings in a dark closet; they find out how plants scatter their seeds by gathering all kinds of seeds and fruits and examining them for hairs, wings, hooks and other devices; they become interested from a new standpoint in the vegetables to which they were introduced the first year and get together all the kinds they can find in the garden and market, grouping them according to the part of the plant that is eaten,—root, leaf, stem, flower or seed.

In the Third Grade, the fall work opens with a continuation of plant propagation. They set out a new strawberry bed and start cuttings in individual pots for the geranium-bed that supplies the school window-boxes. The Third Grade has owned and made a success of the geranium-bed for seven years.

Another line of work dealing with new material in the Third Grade is that of beautifying and caring for the grounds about one's home. While it is true that very few of the children in our school have a city home with a yard of sufficient size to admit of much decoration or landscape-gardening, still many of them have summer homes in the country, and almost without exception they aspire to having some day a home with a yard and garden or better still—a farm. We believe in fostering this healthy and normal ambition to the extent of giving the children of this grade a practical knowledge of shrubs and vines as well as of trees and flowers and so to secure their future independence of the landscape gardener. Perhaps no series of lessons throughout the entire course of nature-study rouses more interest than the study of vines. We begin by going out on the street and into the garden and finding all the vines that we can, with one question only in mind,—"How do vines climb?" We learn that the Japanese ivy climbs by means of tiny suckers, that the bean and morning glory have twining stems, the clematis has twisting leaf-stalks, the English ivy has rootlets, the grape and pumpkin have tendrils, and the crimson rambler has reflexed prickles or "turned-back stickers" as one child put it. This problem involves others, and our next work is to find out what support is needed by each kind of vine. The children discover for themselves that the Japanese ivy grows well only on stone or brick, the English ivy requires soil-filled crevices for its rootlets and does not take kindly to our new American walls, the bean needs a pole, the morning glory a string, the grape a trellis, etc. We discuss the problem of why vines climb and then turn our attention to the uses of vines. Again the children are happy in finding out for themselves that some vines make good shade for a porch, or serve as a screen, or furnish both fruit and shade like the grape, or cover up ugly walls like the Japanese ivy. Then the question of relative beauty is discussed. Seasonal factors enter into this question,—the luxuriant growth of the summer foliage of the moonvine, the brilliant autumn coloring of the woodbine and Japanese ivy, the exquisite purple blossoms of the wistaria in the spring, and the bright berries of the bittersweet in winter. The school-room becomes a place of vines; its walls are gay with bittersweet, and there are pots of English and German ivy on the window-brackets; gorgeous sprays of woodbine are brought in for an art-lesson, and what the children like best of all, the windows are full of individual pots of growing beans. In each pot stands a straight miniature pole a yard high, made by the owner in the hand-work class, and the beans climb up the poles making a fine effect when the pots are placed side by side. The children now work out two more problems: "Where does the vine grow, and how much does it grow in a day?" These questions are solved by marking short spaces of uniform length with India ink along the stem. Frequently the bean-vines blossom and produce very creditable pods of beans.

It is our purpose at the end of the third year to have the children somewhat familiar with such sources of their food, clothing, and shelter as may be found either wild or cultivated within a few miles of New York City. Whatever then comes upon this list is legitimate material for the first three grades.

The work of the Fourth Grade supplements that of the Third Grade by widening the environmental circle so as to include the sources of such things in daily use as cannot be produced or profitably raised near home. We raise or attempt to raise in our school-garden such things as flax, cotton and hemp; wheat, rye, oats and barley; peanuts, tobacco, some of the mints, and the castor-oil plant. If our cotton-bolls are immature and our peanuts small when frost kills the plants, our boys and girls get a practical lesson on the effect of climate. Friends in the south often send us luxuriant plants with bursting bolls of ripe cotton. We place the stunted plants from our own garden beside those from the southern plantation, and with the help of our geographies and encyclopedias work out the causes of the difference. Rainfall, temperature, length of season, soil and altitude are taken into consideration, and the cotton-region of our own country is traced on the map. Plantation life before the sixties is pictured and also present methods of raising cotton. The invention of the cotton-gin and its effect on subsequent history is touched upon, each child having previously tried to separate the cotton from the seeds. In doing this, they make the discovery that cotton serves the same purpose as the hairs of the milkweed seed, namely, as a device for seed dissemination. The effect upon the fiber of cultivation is then explained, and the series of lessons ends with an exhibition of samples of everything made of cotton that can be collected by the children.

Nature-study in the Fifth Grade is confined to two main subjects,—to forestry which occupies the first half of the year, and to the study of birds during the remainder of the time. A more detailed study is made of the trees that the pupils already know something about, and new ones are added to the list. This is largely out-door work. From time to time the New York Botanical Garden has furnished us with valuable material for school-room use. As an aid to tree recognition, we have some years used a key that was made especially for our children and our trees. Always each child is provided with a portfolio and the Mumford pictures of familiar trees as a sort of working basis. To this portfolio they add their leaf collections and other material.

The industrial and aesthetic value of the different trees is dwelt upon, the geographical distribution of our park trees is considered, and our native trees compared as to the length of time that they retain their foliage. One winter month is devoted to the tree from the physiological standpoint. This is no more or less than plant physiology, and the boys and girls become greatly interested in the simple experiments that show absorption, conduction, transpiration, starch-formation, and food-storage. This work is followed by a series of lessons upon the enemies of trees which are of vital interest when one understands that when caterpillars eat the leaves, the manufacture of starch is suspended; that when mice gnaw the bark through the cambium layer, conduction is interfered with; and that when fungi ramify through the pores in the wood of the trunk, they steal the prepared food of the tree or even feed upon its tissue, and so the life of the tree is doomed. It is easy to pass from the individual tree which has now become an organic living thing with its own life-problems to the forest and its problems.

The study of birds has its charms for people of all ages, and a few months devoted to this subject leave our boys and girls with a desire to go on and learn more and more as the years go by. A series of the Mumford pictures illustrating the more common or interesting birds is added to the portfolio, and each child as well as each room starts a bird list. While we are hampered in that it is difficult to take our classes out with profit for the study of wild living birds, still we spend one or more mornings in the Rambles in Central Park, which is acknowledged to be one of the finest centers for the study of migrating birds in the country, and we visit the birds in the Zoological Garden as a class, in groups or individually. To teach our pupils the intelligent use of the museums, public gardens, and other opportunities provided by the city, is one of the aims of our department.

From these brief notes it will be seen that our work has a large element of "doing"; that we are trying to teach our children to interpret nature for themselves; that we are starting them on lines of work that they can follow up individually; that we are providing them with happy and healthful out-door employment and recreation for afternoons, holidays, summer vacations, and for leisure throughout life; that through a love and appreciation of the beautiful they are led to protect and to help nature,—to protect the birds and wild flowers and to care for the parks; that they are led to judge intelligently of the values of life and to destroy (as tenderly as may be) the pests and those forms of life that are injurious or destructive to higher or more valuable species.

Our work is never quite the same for any two years. Some subjects have been eliminated after being tried out; others are temporarily dropped or omitted from lack of time, while new ones are experimented upon and added from time to time. In the outline that follows, no single year has seen the completion of all lines of work in every grade, but these are the subjects that have proved of most value to us.

FIRST GRADE

Plant-life:

Flowers. Learn to recognize the following—

In the fall:

Wild: Goldenrod, Aster, Queen's Lace, Butter and Eggs.

Cultivated: Pansy, Geranium, Morning-glory, Sunflower, Marigold, Zinnia, Nasturtium, California Poppy, Salvia, and Chrysanthemum.

In the spring:

> Wild: Spring Beauty, Hepatica, Blood-root, Adder's Tongue, Violet—blue, white, and yellow, Dandelion, Jack-in-Pulpit, Marsh Marigold, Daisy, Buttercup, and Clover.

Seeds: Collect several kinds from the garden and put away carefully for the spring-planting.

Trees: Oak, Maple, Willow, Chestnut; Pine and Fir (Christmas).

Vegetables: Learn the names of the common vegetables and find out how they grow in the garden; visit a grocer's window where vegetables are displayed and learn how they get from the farmer to the grocer. (Thanksgiving)

Bulbs: The last of October, plant hyacinths in individual pots; visit them once or twice during winter in their underground quarters; bring into school-room in time to blossom for Easter; take home for an Easter present to mother. Plant a bed of hyacinths in the garden to send to sick children when they blossom.

The Pumpkin—a Hallowe'en subject: study it as a "seed-box"; save and clean the seeds; put away in individual envelopes made by the children; make the pumpkin into a Jack-o-lantern; in the spring, plant the seeds in individual pots and keep in the school-room; plant in three ways to determine if growth is affected.

How plants get ready for winter: Study the trees and grass on the campus, the vegetables and flowers in the garden to find out.

The Garden: In the spring make a flower-garden; learn to use hoe and rake; plant Marigolds, Pansies, Nasturtiums, Zinnias, Salvia, and California Poppy (flowers showy and seeds large).

Animal-life:

The Rabbit: Keep in large cage in school-room for a week or more; care for and feed carefully; let children work out simple problems like the following.—Why does the rabbit make a good pet? How does he take care of himself? What can we do to make him happy?

The Pigeon: Keep in school-room and study like the rabbit.

The Robin: Song, nest, eggs, use to us.

Gold-fish: Keep in aquarium; set up the aquarium ("fish-home") in school-room before the children.

Butterflies and Moths: In fall, bring in caterpillars, watch formation of cocoons; try to bring out for Easter.

How do animals get ready for winter?

Physical phenomena: From time to time, note color of sky, presence of clouds, fog, snow, rain, ice, sleet, frost, wind, etc.

Children of this grade visit a farm and a market.

SECOND GRADE

Plant-life

Flowers. Review those learned in Grade I and add the following:

In the fall:

Wild: Clovers,—red, white, yellow or hop, buffalo; Gentians,—fringed and closed, Cardinal flower, Yarrow.

Cultivated: Sweet Alyssum, Mignonette, Petunia, Verbena, Ageratum, Phlox, Portulaca, Coxcomb, Cosmos, Snapdragon, Bachelor's Button, Calendula.

In the spring:

Wild: Saxifrage, Wild Lily-of-the-Valley, Solomon's Seal. Rock Pink, Dutchman's Breeches, Bellwort, Toothwort, Dogwood, Azalea.

How are the spring flowers able to get into bloom so quickly?

What becomes of the plants after blossoming? Develop idea of food-making and food-storage by the plant.

Trees: Review those already learned and add Sweet Gum, Horsechestnut, Elm and Lombardy Poplar. Study outlines of trees; cut in paper.

Evergreen Trees: Compare Pine, Fir, Spruce and Hemlock with reference to value for Christmas trees.

Seed-dispersal: Collect as many kinds of seeds and fruits as possible; supplement from school-collections; discuss agency and device for dissemination.

Bulbs: Plant Daffodils in individual pots for Easter; plant a bed in the garden for the children in St. Luke's Hospital.

Vegetables: Study with reference to the part of the plant they represent, e.g., root, stem, leaf, flower, fruit or seed. (Thanksgiving)

Germination: Plant beans between blotting-paper and glass in common tumblers; compare to determine most favorable amount of water; note cessation of growth and determine the cause. Plant other seeds,—Corn, Pea, Grass, Mustard, etc., in same way; keep some in dark; note effect on size of seed of light and darkness, of heat and cold.

The Garden: In the spring, plant a bed of radishes and make a flower-garden; plant Mignonette, Sweet Alyssum, Verbenas, Petunias, Portulaca, Snapdragon, Bachelor's Button and Calendula; sow extremely small seeds broadcast.

Animal-life:

English Sparrow: Study sparrows on street; are they a nuisance or of value to us?

Grackles and Starlings on Campus: Compare Crow and Blue Jay; note return of Robin, Bluebird and Song Sparrow.

The Squirrel: Study squirrels on Campus; find out what they eat, how they gnaw, where they sleep. Compare the Chipmunk and Red Squirrel.

Garden Foes: injurious insects,—plant-lice, scales, caterpillars.

Garden Friends: the earth-worm and toad. What does the toad do for us? What can we do for the toad? Compare the frog. Keep tadpoles in aquaria.

Physical Nature-Study:

The three forms of water; swelling of water in ice-formation, applications; simple experiments in evaporation; effect of frost on soil, on rocks.

The thermometer: value to the gardener.

Building-stones: Granite, Marble, Sandstone and Slate.

Common minerals: Mica, Quartz, Flint, Chalk.

Three illustrated lectures on "Spring," "Winter" and "Autumn" are given in this grade.

THIRD GRADE

The Garden:

Fall work:

Plant propagation:

Strawberry-bed: Study the bed planted by Grade III last year; find original plants; select strongest of new plants and make a new bed; each child should transplant at least one plant.

Geranium-bed: From geranium-bed made by Grade III of last year, select cuttings and plant in individual pots; keep in greenhouse till blossoms appear, then transfer to school-room; in spring transplant to the garden-bed to be used for window-boxes in fall and to furnish the next Third Grade class with cuttings.

The Potato: Study in fall; "make starch"; cut properly and plant in individual pots in greenhouse; "dig" in spring. Potato-beetle.

Radishes: Plant individual boxes of radishes in greenhouse; use different kinds of seeds; decide which is best for greenhouse cultivation.

Seed-formation: Study vegetable garden with reference to seed-formation; annuals, biennials and perennials.

Spring work:

Plan the kitchen-garden on paper; order seeds; mark off beds to correspond to plan; plant about fifteen kinds of vegetables in the most approved way. Coöperative work.

The Yard:

The Lawn: Make a lawn in a window-box; sow seed, trim carefully and determine where growth takes place.

Enemies of the lawn:

The Mole: structure and habits.

The June-bug: metamorphosis.

The Grasshopper: compare with June-bug.

Flowering Shrubs: Forsythia, Japanese Quince, Bridal Wreath, Syringa, Lilac, Althea, Barberry, etc. Study with reference to beauty of form, value for hedge, beauty of foliage or flower or color-mass, bright berries or fruits for attraction of birds.

Vines: Japanese Ivy, English Ivy, Woodbine, Grape, Moon-vine, Clematis, Honeysuckle, Morning-glory, Scarlet Runner, Virginia Creeper, etc., mode of climbing,—twining stem, tendrils, rootlets, etc.; needed support; value for shade, screen or wall-covering; beauty of foliage, flower or autumn coloring; value for fruit.

Trees: Review those learned in preceding grades and add Tulip-tree, Sycamore, Catalpa, Linden, Cottonwood and Beech. Consider value for shade, screen, wind-break or beauty of form, and autumn coloring. Note advantage for single trees, clumps or avenues.

The Orchard: Native fruit-trees, the apple, pear, peach, quince.

Nut-bearing trees (native): Hickory, Black Walnut, Butternut, Beech, Chestnut.

Insect-pests in orchard; bird-friends.

Hive of Bees: Structure of the bee; queen, worker, drone; gathering of honey, pollen; wax; care of eggs and young.

Paper-wasp, Mud-dauber, Ants. Compare with bee. Keep colony of ants in school-room.

The parts of a flower; function of each; mutual dependence of bees and flowers.

The Beaver and other fur-bearing animals. Visit beaver-dam in Zoological Garden.

The Sea-gull: value as a scavenger.

Group all the animals and plants studied thus far into ecological groups; make window-gardens or sand-table demonstrations of one or more of the following,—swamp, brook and its banks, sunny upland slope, rocky exposed hillside, ravine, pine woods, deciduous woods; sink pans for water; use animal pictures or labels; develop an idea of the country in the time of Hudson.

Illustrated lectures on " The Fauna and Flora in the Time of Hudson," and "Domestic Animals and Their Wild Relatives."

FOURTH GRADE

Agriculture

Garden-work:

Kitchen-garden; gather the vegetables planted the preceding spring.

The Grains: Harvest the Wheat, Rye, Oats, Barley and Corn. Plant a bed of winter Rye,—sow one-half in drills and one-half broadcast to determine the best way of sowing.

Fiber Plants: Gather the Flax, Cotton, Jute and Hemp; supplement with material and pictures to illustrate industrial processes.

Peanuts: Compare method of growth with peas, with nuts.

Sweet Potato: Compare with common potato; grow one in water.

Tobacco: Note method of growth.

Castor-oil Plant: Rub broken seeds on paper to show oil.

Rubber: Use large school-room plant; slash in places and collect and dry the sap.

Sugar: Maple, Beet, Cane; study with help of specimens, pictures and experience.

The Products of the Zones: Collect and arrange material on three shelves representing Tropical, Temperate and Cold Regions; include:

Tea, Coffee, Cocoa;

Spices of all kinds;

Fruits such as the Banana, Pineapple, Orange, Lemon, Grape-fruit, imported Grapes, the Fig, Date and Olive;

Nuts such as the Brazil-nut, English Walnut, Pecan, Filbert and Cocoanut.

Supplement with charts and pictures showing culture and manner of growth. (Thanksgiving)

Lumbering:

Pine, Spruce, Hemlock, White Cedar, Red Cedar; value and uses. (Christmas)

Lumber camps: Saw-mills,—site, management and power; transportation of logs and lumber; the lumber-yard.

Fisheries:

Fish of the Coast, of the Hudson, of mountain-streams; methods of fishing.

Salmon: study as the type of the fish.

Lobster; development, necessity of protection. Use Cray-fish for individual study.

Clam and Oyster; the Star-fish an enemy of the Oyster.

Turtle, French Snails: keep alive in school-room.

Dragon-fly and Caddis-fly: keep nymphs in fresh-water aquarium (use material to illustrate Kingsley's "Water-Babies").

Salt-water aquarium: illustrate life of the seashore as far as practicable.

Mining and Quarrying.   (This line of work is done largely by the departments of Geography and Industrial Arts)

Soils: Clay, sand, gravel; lime, salines and alkaline substances; fertility, sources of humus; barrenness,—causes of, deserts; water-content; simple experiments showing comparative water-content of different soils; experiments showing effect of fertile and barren soils on plant-growth.

Minerals and Metals in common use.

Methods of mining.

Manufacture of Glass and Porcelain.

Stones used for building purposes, monuments, paving.

Visit a quarry or excavation for foundation of building.

An illustrated lecture on each of the above main topics completes the work in nature-study for the fourth grade.

FIFTH GRADE

Recognition at all seasons of the following list of park and forest trees; their native habitat; value for lumber, shade, windbreak or ornament:

Maples: Sugar, Red, White, Norway, Sycamore, Japanese,
Sweet-gum, Sycamore or Plane-tree, Tulip-tree,
Poplars: Silver, Lombardy, Cottonwood, Balm-of-Gilead,
Catalpa, Linden or Basswood, Elm, Beech, Chestnut, Willow,
Birches: Black, Yellow or Curly, Gray, White, Weeping,
Honey Locust, Common Locust, Ailanthus, Ash, **Horsechest**-nut,
Shag-bark Hickory, Pignut, Black Walnut, Butternut,
Pine, Spruce, Hemlock, Balsam Fir, Juniper, Red and White Cedar.

Dissemination of trees from seeds, shoots or cuttings; agents of and devices for seed-dispersal.

Planting of acorns and maple seeds; transplanting of seedlings or young trees to country homes; rooting and planting of willow-branches.

The Tree as an Individual: its life-problems and how it meets them; structure and functions of the different parts of the tree,—the roots and root-hairs, trunk with the heart-wood, sap-wood, cambium, inner and outer bark; branches and twigs, buds, leaves, flowers, fruits and seeds. This work is illustrated by an abundance of material, microscopic slides, stereopticon views, transparent wood-sections, blocks cut to show the grain, and a series of simple physiological experiments to show absorption, conduction, transpiration and starch formation.

The Forest and its Problems: the forest-floor, undergrowth and canopy; effect on rain-fall; value and uses of the forest, its care and preservation; care of injured or diseased trees; reforestation; legislation concerning forests; government reservations.

Enemies of the Forest:

Fungi, their work and life-history.

Winds, Storms, Lightning, Snow, Ice, Sleet.

Fires, causes and prevention.

Gnawing animals: Rabbits, Mice, the Beaver.

Grazing animals: Deer, Cattle, Sheep.

Insects: Moths,—the Gypsy, Brown-tail, Tussock, Tent Caterpillar; Plant-lice or Aphides, Scales, Elm-leaf Beetle. Life-histories of injurious insects and methods of dealing with them; substances used for and ways of spraying and fumigation.

Man, the careless or ignorant or avaricious lumberman.

Friends of the Forest: Birds. (Not only the relation of birds to trees but also to the garden, to crops and to vegetation in general is here considered.)

The Bird as an Individual: its structure and life-history; structural and color adaptations; habits; nest, eggs and young; food and consequent value to man. Something is learned of all the birds on the following list: English Sparrow, Starling, Grackle, Junco, Chickadee, Nuthatch, Brown Creeper, Song Sparrow, Red-winged Blackbird, Robin, Bluebird, Cedar Waxwing, Crossbill, Meadowlark, Kingbird, Baltimore Oriole, Goldfinch, Cardinal, Scarlet Tanager, Indigo Bunting, Vireo, Humming-bird, Flicker, Downy Woodpecker, Blue Jay, Crow, Cuckoo, Whip-poor-will, Purple Martin, Cliff and Barn Swallows, a few game-birds, the Seagull, an owl, hawk and heron.

Migration: Permanent and summer residents, winter and transient visitants; causes and routes of migration.

Bird-lists are kept,—both class and individual.

The material consists of pictures, mounted birds with nests and as many live birds as we are able to see.

Visits are made to the American Museum of Natural History, to the Zoological Garden and to "The Rambles" in Central Park.

Four illustrated lectures on trees and birds are given in this grade.

SIXTH GRADE

GENERAL SCIENCE

Up to the Sixth Grade the study of nature has consisted mainly of lessons based on zoölogy and botany. In the Sixth Grade general science is made the basis of the course of study, the topics for discussion being selected largely from the fields of physics, astronomy, biology, chemistry, and geography. In choosing topics much care has been taken to find those which particularly appeal to the child, and which serve to explain in a simple way a number of modern mechanisms, mechanical devices, works of municipal engineering, and such phenomena of the child's environment as especially arouse his interest.

Two thirty-minute periods each week are devoted to this instruction, and the experiments or demonstrations connected with it are first introduced in the laboratory period. The discussion of the problem and of the experiments constitutes the second lesson. The purpose is to start with a problem concerning which the children are seeking information; observation, demonstration, and information from books and articles assist in the assembling of facts; explanations and applications follow.

The type of subject matter is changed somewhat from year to year in the effort to find the material best serving the needs of the children of this grade.

Some of the problems taken up are suggested in the following outline:

I. How does New York City get its water supply?
  1. The Old Croton Aqueduct.
  2. The New Croton Aqueduct.
  3. The Catskill Aqueduct.
  4. Problems in physics connected with the question.
    a. How does a siphon work?
    b. What makes anything have weight?
    c. In what direction does water pressure act?
    d. How much pressure does it exert?
    e. In preparation for siphoning the water under the Hudson River, how did the engineers know in what direction the drill inclined?
    f. How did they know how deep to go?
  5. Problems related to getting a pure water supply.

II. What makes engines go?
  1. What are the principal parts of an engine?
  2. How was the steam engine developed?
  3. What is the effect of heat on gases? Liquids? Solids?
  4. In what particulars is a gasoline engine different from a steam engine?

III. The balloon, the airship, the aeroplane.
  1. How does each work?
  2. What were the problems connected with the development of each?
  3. For what is each especially fitted?
  4. How can an airman tell how high in the air he is?— The barometer.
  5. What questions are yet unsolved in connection with each?

IV. Divers (and Submarines).
  1. How are they able to go down below the surface of the water?

2. How do they get air when under water?
3. How far down can they go?
4. What do they do when they want to come up?
5. How can they tell where it is safe to come up?
6. Of what use are they?
7. What is a diving bell? What is it used for? How were the Hudson and East River tunnels made?

V. How are musical tones produced?

VI. Electric lamps, electric heating devices, wireless telegraph.
1. How do electric wires light lamps?
   a. How does the current flow?
   b. What are the different kinds of lamps?
   c. What is meant by Volts? Amperes? Watts?
2. How does an electric wire heat?
3. How does the wireless telegraph work?

VII. Astronomy.
1. What is the sun?
2. How does the moon differ from the sun?
3. How is it that the moon affects the tides?
4. What is the difference between a star and a planet?
5. What are shooting stars?
6. Why do we see more shooting stars at certain seasons than at others?
7. Where did those meteorites that are in the Museum of Natural History come from?
8. Are we likely to be killed by meteors?

VIII. What are earthquakes?
1. What causes them?
2. Why do they occur in some places and not in others?
3. What happens if they occur in the sea?

IX. Why is fresh air so necessary to our health?
1. Why is exercise in the open air so valuable?
2. Why is oxygen important to the blood? To the digestion?
3. How does oxygen keep us warm?
4. How can we keep the air in our rooms fresh?

X. Our eyes and their care.

    1. How do we see?

    2. Why are eyes of different colors?

    3. Why is the pupil of the eye larger in a dim light and smaller in a bright light? How is it that a cat can see in the dark?

    4. How should we care for the eyes?

REFERENCES:

Inventors at Work. George Iles. Doubleday, Page and Company.

An Air Line over Germany. *World's Work*, November, 1912.

Harper's Electricity Book for Boys. Joseph H. Adams. Harper and Brothers.

Electricity for Young People. Tudor Jenks. Frederick A. Stokes Company.

Electricity and Its Everyday Uses. John F. Woodhull. (The Children's Library of Work and Play.) Doubleday, Page and Company.

Boy's Book of New Inventions. H. E. Maule. Doubleday, Page and Company.

Nature's Miracles. Elisha Gray. 3 vols. Fords, Howard and Hulbert, New York.

The Children's Book of Stars. G. E. Mitton. Adam & Chas. Black, London.

Monthly Magazines:

Popular Electricity.

Popular Mechanics.

The Mechanical World.

SOURCES:

Town and City. Frances Gulick Jewett. (Gulick Hygiene Series.) Ginn and Company.

The Deepest Siphon Tunnel in the World. Robert K. Tomlin, Jr. *Scribner's Monthly*, May, 1912.

Book of Knowledge. The Grolier Society, New York.

General Science. Bertha M. Clark. American Book Company.

General Science. Percy Rowell. The Macmillan Company.

Boy's Book of Inventions. R. S. Baker. Doubleday and McClure Company.

Story of Great Inventions. E. E. Burns. Harper and Brothers.

Stories of Useful Inventions. S. E. Forman. The Century Company.

INDUSTRIAL ARTS

The purpose of the work in industrial arts is to give the pupils a background of knowledge and experience which will enable them to appreciate the industrial aspects of modern civilization. Just as the work in geography, history, or arithmetic aims to put the child in touch with those aspects of his environment, so this work in industrial arts is an attempt to bring the child into sympathetic and intelligent relationship with the world of industry in which he lives.

Knowledge and appreciation in this field, is gained through actual constructive work, explanations, discussions, demonstrations, and excursions. It is believed that the knowledge and appreciation which is most vital to the child, and which interests and appeals to him most, is gained through the constructive work, so in all the grades more time is given to this phase than to any other. This is particularly true of the work in the early grades. The work is organized so as to afford the pupils manipulative work in practically all the materials used in modern society to meet the primal needs of man. The industrial content consists, for the most part, of facts relative to the materials used, their sources and preparation, the simple technical processes by which these materials are transformed into useful products, and the study of the workers as productive individuals in the community. Thus an industrial attitude or viewpoint is developed, resulting in an appreciation of an interest in the world's work.

The pupils are led to recognize and think of the things which serve their needs—food, shelter, and clothing—as the products of industry, the materials of which they are made as the materials of industry, and the workers who devote their time to constructing these things as large contributors to human welfare. It is a new viewpoint for the child when he realizes that clay, for example, which he has known as a play material, has a real use and value in the life world; that the making of things with it occupies a great many people every day, with the result that he has dishes from which to eat his food, ornaments with which to beautify his home, and a brick house to live in.

Aside from the general information gained relative to the materials of industry, the work of the artisans, and skill in processes of manipulation, appreciation and love of the beautiful are also gained, thus functioning directly in the development of good taste and ability to choose wisely the industrial products which are required in our homes in meeting our daily needs.

The general purpose of the course in industrial arts may be summarized under the three following heads:

1. To develop appreciation leading to the intelligent selection and use of the various industrial products which are fundamental to the primal needs of man.

2. To acquire sufficient skill in the various industrial processes to construct a project pleasing to the pupil, and illustrative of the industry.

3. To develop an appreciation and understanding of the social and economic setting of industry in society, and also an intelligent basis for the further study of industrial problems.

The aims thus set forth are realized through a study of the following industries: clay, concrete, textile, wood, paper, printing, and metal. Aside from the work given to clarify ideas relative to these industries, opportunity is provided for free manipulative work from the standpoint of expression. Under this phase of the course are grouped the holiday and illustrative work of the lower grades, and the after-school shop work of the Sixth and Seventh grades.

The construction of projects in the various materials enumerated forms a basis for the acquisition of skill in manipulation, and for the development of industrial concepts. Owing to the varying local and individual interests, there is some diversity of projects from year to year, but the basic principles for selecting these projects remain the same:

1. Projects must be of real and vital interest to the child, and present a problematic situation which he can solve.

2. Projects must be so selected as to permit of systematic development and successful achievement of the manipulative processes.

3. Projects must, so far as possible, illustrate or typify modern industrial processes.

4. Projects must be so selected as to allow some opportunity for individuality in structural or decorative design.

The relation of the industrial work to the study of New York City is set forth graphically in the chart under the geography course. The general method of procedure is to study first the industries in their broad relation to human life. With this as a background the local setting of the industry is then studied in detail, developing such topics as the extent and local importance of the industry, the conditions under which the industry is pursued, and the general personal and community problems resulting from mal-adjustments of the industry to the welfare of the worker.

GRADES I, II, III, IV, AND V

The boys and girls work together in the first five grades, and follow practically the same course throughout. In the First and Second grades the work, with the exception of that in wood, is done in the class room. Much of the work is planned in conference with the grade teacher, because of the close relation which exists between it and the other lines of school work. All the work is supervised by the special teacher, and at least one lesson a week in each grade is taught by her. The grade teacher, with the help of the industrial art assistant, takes charge of the other two lessons. In the Third, Fourth, and Fifth grades, all the work is done in the hand-work room and is taught by the special teacher. In all the grades the work in fine and industrial arts is very closely related, as many of the projects are designed in the former and carried out in the latter. Ninety minutes a week in thirty-minute periods are given to the subject during the first and second years, and eighty minutes a week in forty-minute periods during the third, fourth, and fifth years.

The work develops from a consideration of the common needs of the individual for food, clothing, and shelter, and involves a study of the clay, concrete, paper, wood, textiles, and food industries as the means whereby these necessities of life are supplied. The study of an industry consists of the purely informational work and the manipulative work. Both are represented in each grade (this is not true of every industry, at present, but will be in the course of time), the former occupying comparatively little of the time in the First Grade, and increasing gradually in proportion as the grades advance. The children are very much interested in the purely informational side, when it is presented to them simply and clearly. They are especially interested when pictures can be secured, or visits made, to clarify their ideas. Many of the children have traveled, and have visited factories of various kinds in different places, so that they are frequently able to add to the pleasure and interest of the class by telling of their experiences. The children's chief interest, however, is in the doing and in the object they are making as an end in itself. No special division of time for the two parts of the work is made, as is the case in the upper grades. From time to time a whole or part of a period is used for discussion, or the oral or written reproduction of a subject which has been discussed. Some of this reproduction work forms a part of the work in English.

In the First Grade the special object is to establish a point of view or general industrial attitude toward the everyday things the children have, rather than to accumulate any amount of knowledge or to develop technique. The children are introduced to various industries and industrial materials, and learn a few simple facts about them, for example, as to sources—that cotton comes from a plant and wool from sheep. The work is, of course, closely related to the lives and experiences of the children.

In the Second Grade, some of the primitive aspects are considered through the study of Indian life, while from the Third Grade on the work develops more definitely along industrial lines.

For the sake of being able to follow more readily the study of a specific material through a series of grades, the work with clay may be described as follows.

The following story, made by the First Grade children, will serve to show the beginnings.

Clay is a sticky kind of dirt.
Clay is different colors.
Miss Weiser showed us a block of colored clay.
The colors were red, white, gray, yellow. and brown.
Some Indians dug this clay out of a clay bank, and made it into a cube.
Clay must be wet before it is used.
We use many things made of clay,—china dishes, china ornaments, bricks, and flower-pots.
Many people work in factories every day to make these things of clay.
Things made of clay must be baked before they can be used.
We saw the oven where our clay things are baked.

In the Second Grade, the study of clay as a material is carried a little further, and the children learn what has been done to prepare the clay for use before it comes to them, and see pictures of the machines used. They also take some lumps of dry clay and make it ready for use by going through similar operations by hand. They visit the kiln and learn more about it. They make a tile and learn the use of a wooden mold in shaping wet clay, also how dry clay is used to make the small floor tiles with which all New York children are very familiar. A study of Indian pottery is made, and the method of coiling tried. Clay as a building material is then introduced in the making of the pueblo.

In the Third Grade, the study of this material is continued. It is learned that clay is a kind of soil made by the decomposition of particular rocks, and that there are different grades of clay which have various uses. The children tell of their experiences in finding and identifying clay in the country and elsewhere. They make a flower-pot, and afterward see one shaped on the potter's wheel.

The use of clay in buildings is further developed. This leads to a study of the brick-making industry, taking up the various processes, the machinery used, and ending with a brief historical sketch and survey of the industry as it exists in this country at present. and especially in New York State and in the Hudson River Valley. While making this study, they construct bricks in molds and build the walls of a small brick house (see illustration) using tiles of their own to build a fireplace.

In the Fourth Grade, the composition of clay is considered. and the subject of kilns, their firing, stacking, and temperature cones is referred to. Some modern ways of making dishes—jollying or jigging, and pressing—as well as firing, decorating, and glazing are studied. A plate is made to illustrate some of these processes. The terra cotta industry is also taken up, and some artificial stone is made for the brick house.

In the Fifth Grade, the children make more artistic pieces of pottery. In this connection they learn about the composition and mixing of glazes, the tests of colors, the action of fire on glazes, the processes of shaping in plaster molds by lining the mold and pouring, and how a plaster mold is constructed. On the informational side they gather a few important facts about the history of pottery making, the industry as it exists to-day, the number and location of the principal factories, the capital invested, and the conditions under which the laborers work. The children also become acquainted with the values and characteristics of typical American and European wares. Glass making as a closely related industry is briefly considered.

The following is a more detailed outline of all the work of each grade.

GRADE I

INDUSTRIES: CLAY, PAPER, TEXTILES, AND WOOD

Clay.

Source, uses, and main characteristics.

Processes involved in making things of clay, as shaping, drying, firing (visit kiln), and glazing.

Manipulative Work: Toy dishes and ornaments for doll house, marbles, paper weights, and trays, involving the operations of rolling and rubbing to prepare the clay, and tapping and pressing to shape it. Most of the things made in this grade are shaped from one piece of clay. Each article is the result of one lesson's work, though the children may try several times on the same thing. No tools are used. The paper weights and trays are sometimes decorated by pressing pumpkin seeds into the clay, while it is soft, to form patterns, the latter having been made beforehand in the art class. After this the objects are glazed by the children of the Fourth and Fifth grades according to the colors chosen by the makers. Plasticine is used for modeling the orange or grape fruit, lemon, and tangerine. This precedes the cutting and drawing of the same in the art work.

Pottery.   Grades I to V.

Paper.

Uses.   Of what made.

Manipulative Work: Papering doll house and making simple booklets and ornaments for the Christmas tree, involving folding, cutting, and pasting.

Textiles.

Uses and sources of wool, silk, cotton, and linen.

Identification of wool and silk: Children cannot tell linen and cotton apart, but can distinguish both from wool and silk.

Main processes: Twisting into thread, weaving, knitting, making clothing, cutting pattern, sewing (hand and machine), fitting.

Manipulative Work: Curtains, rugs, etc., for doll house, hammock for doll, and reed work basket with wooden bottom.

Wood.

Uses and source.

Main processes in wood construction: sawing, planing, nailing, and staining.

Principal tools: saw, plane, hammer, etc.

Manipulative Work: Loom frame, hammock stand, and doll furniture, involving measuring and nailing. Some of the measuring is done as a part of the arithmetic work.

Illustrative Work. Group projects:

Farm scene. Eskimo village. Different stories, or scenes from stories.

Busy Work: Knitting on toy knitters, weaving mats and other articles on cardboard looms (circular), and making horse reins of cord.

Modeling in clay and plasticine.

GRADE II

INDUSTRIES: CLAY, PAPER, TEXTILES AND WOOD

Clay.

Review of work of First Grade.

Main processes in preparing clay for use: digging, grinding, sifting, mixing with water, and pressing. Pictures of machinery used.

Visit to our kiln: Of what materials made, fuel used, general principles of operation, time required for firing our clay.

Use of molds in shaping clay.

Tile making industry. Use of dry clay.

Indian pottery. Building by coiling.

Manipulative Work: Fern dishes, tiles (in wooden molds), bowls (Indian), Jack-o-lanterns, snowmen, and Indian beads, involving same operations as in First Grade, with kneading clay, filling a mold, and slip painting (design on tile) added.

Model apple and pear in round. Draw same in group (on clay tile) and model very slightly.

Textiles.

Primitive cloth, skins and bark, patterns painted on.

Our printed cloths; kinds.

Needles; primitive and modern.

Use of skins in our clothing: shoes, gloves, furs, and hats (felt).

Knitted goods: Indian loom, shuttle, warp, woof.

Wood Work.   Grades I and II.

Manipulative Work: Indian suits (print cloth), book-mark, shoe-bag and Indian rug or blanket, involving sewing, plain and very simple pattern weaving and crocheting.

Wood.

Different kinds of wood.

Names of some common woods.

Main processes in lumbering, felling, sawing into planks; lumber yards.

Manipulative Work: Bows and arrows, ring-toss game, bean-bag board, and tile molds, involving measuring, squaring, sawing, boring, nailing, and gluing.

Tools: Try-square, back saw, mitre box, hammer and brace and bit.

Illustrative Work. Group projects: Indian village. Robinson Crusoe. Pueblo. Theatre.

Busy Work:

Cross-stitch mat, reed basket (wooden bottom), rugs, and crocheting.

GRADE III

INDUSTRIES: CLAY, PAPER, TEXTILES AND WOOD

Clay.

More detailed study of clay as a material.

Soil and its formation, rocks which produce clay—feldspar. Different grades of clay—kaolin. Characteristic differences between clay and other kinds of soil. Experiences in finding and identifying clay, both wet and dry. Stories about discovery of use of clay. "Grandma Kaolin" story.

Bungalow. Grades III, IV, and V.
Brick Work—Grade III.
Terra Cotta—Grade IV.
Concrete and Plastering—Grade V.
Framework—Grades III, IV, and V.

Potter's wheel as a method of shaping clay. Demonstration of the making of a flower-pot on wheel.

Clay as a building material. Brick making: processes, machines, a typical brickyard, and its clay banks. Brick industry in this country as to cost and kinds and quantities of

bricks produced. The Hudson Valley as a brick-making
center; the state which leads in this industry.

Brief historical sketch of brick making. The story of the
Children of Israel. Primitive brick making.

Brick laying: how bricks are placed in a wall. mortar and
tools used. The use of bricks for paving.

New York City as a market for bricks. Brick houses having an
iron structure. Watch some building being built. The
Building Department of New York City; some of its simple
requirements for safety.

Bungalow. Interior View.

Manipulative Work: Flower-pots and saucers, bricks and tiles
for the bungalow, and art tiles. The following operations are
added in this grade: working to a given height. hammering
a layer of clay to a given thickness, the use of the tool in
cutting clay, glazing the fireplace tiles, tracing designs on
art tiles. and painting either the design or the background
with colored slip.

Laying brick walls and tile fireplace in bungalow. (The art tiles are glazed with a colorless glaze by children of the Fourth or Fifth grades.)

Art modeling. Rosette or flower form in relief, with simple modeling of petals. This requires more than one lesson and involves a new use of the tool in removing the background. This work follows the drawing of flowers in the art class.

Paper.

Making of box with fitted cover at Christmas time, simple booklets for mounting pictures, and similar articles.

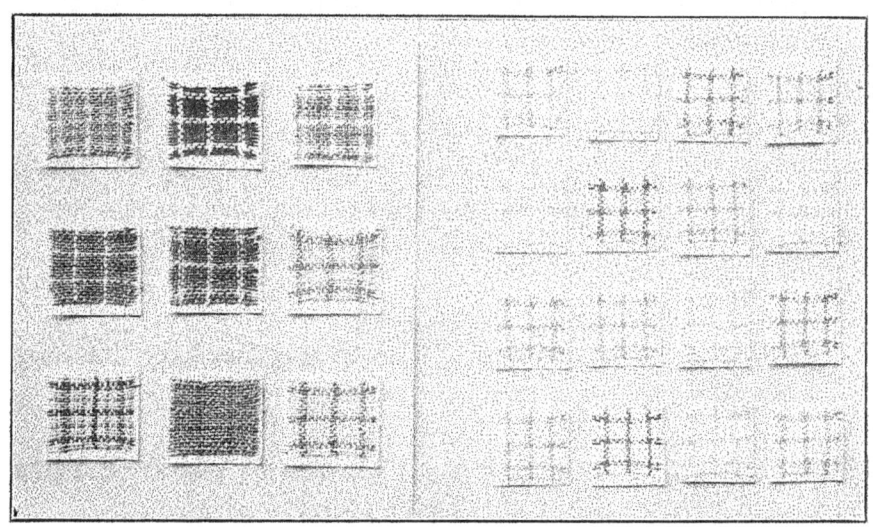

Study in Cloth Design—Plaids. Grade III.

Textiles. Animal fibres; wool and silk.

Wool.

Sheep and other wool-bearing animals.

Wool as a fibre, processes of preparation, shearing, washing, carding, spinning. Machines used. Demonstration of carding by hand, and spinning on wheel.

Sheep-raising countries; sheep raising in United States. Very brief historical sketch. Bible references. Story of Jason and Golden Fleece from "Tanglewood Tales."

Manufacture of woolen goods in the United States.

Silk.

The silk worm.

The silk thread; processes of preparation, machines used.

Silk-producing countries.

Stories of the origin of silk. Brief historical sketch. · Silk manufacture in the United States.

New York City as a market for silk and woolen goods.

Cloth weaving and the continuous warp loom.

The selvedge; color designs. Mixed, striped, and plaid cloths.

Manipulative Work:

Shear, wash, card and spin wool by hand.

Weave strip of cloth on continuous warp loom and make into bag or scarf.

Make needle-case of canvas embroidered in cross-stitch and backstitch (lettering), or card-case of linen.

Wood.

Saws, sawmills; visit carpenter shop at Teachers College.

Manipulative Work: Assist in cutting and laying the flooring, and cutting shingles for bungalow.

Make brick molds, and continuous warp looms.

Busy Work:

Cross-stitch, weaving, crocheting.

A play store or market made of wooden box. A circus wagon.

The following is a typical paper written by one of the pupils in connection with the work of this grade.

PROCESSES IN BRICK MAKING

Have you ever wondered where the bricks in your house come from? They have a long story. First they were nothing but clay in clay banks. At last it was taken in carts to the brick factory. The clay had to be cleaned, of course, but the main processes in making are shaping or molding, drying and firing. You can make bricks by hand or machinery, but they have to go through these three processes.

GRADE IV

INDUSTRIES: CLAY, TEXTILES, AND WOOD

Clay.

Pottery industry; the making of china dishes. Clays used, composition of kaolin clay as a mixture of materials. Potters' secret factory processes in making china dishes, methods of decoration, glazing, and firing. Kilns. Special study of our kiln; its structure and operation; telling temperature by cones; what happens to clay under fire. Biscuit firing, glaze firing, stacking and temperature for each.

Building uses of clay. Stones commonly used for building. Quarrying. Clay as a substitute for stone; appearance, strength, fire tests. The terra cotta industry. Hollow tile; its manufacture and use.

Manipulative Work:

Plates and terra cotta pieces for bungalow. The former involves the use of a plaster mold.

Art modeling. Vegetable forms in round, and built up half round on tiles.

Textiles.

Detailed study of two principal vegetable fibres (cotton and linen) as to growth, processes of preparation for use and machinery (inventors). Supply, New York City as a market. The clothing industry in New York City. Minor vegetable fibres and their uses. Simple woven designs; diagonal and figured cloth. Foot looms, power looms. Names and prices of principal kinds of cotton and linen cloth.

Rug and carpet weaving.

Knitted goods.

Manipulative Work:

Weave diagonal and spot designs.

Make necessary furnishings for toy apartment.

Weave large rugs on hand looms and class rug on foot loom.

Weave sofa pillow covers in diagonal and spot designs.

Knitting.

Wood.

Lumbering; its processes.

Structure of wood; fibres, grain.

Hard and soft woods; supply.

Manufacture of furniture (general).

Sandpapering and staining.

Manipulative Work:

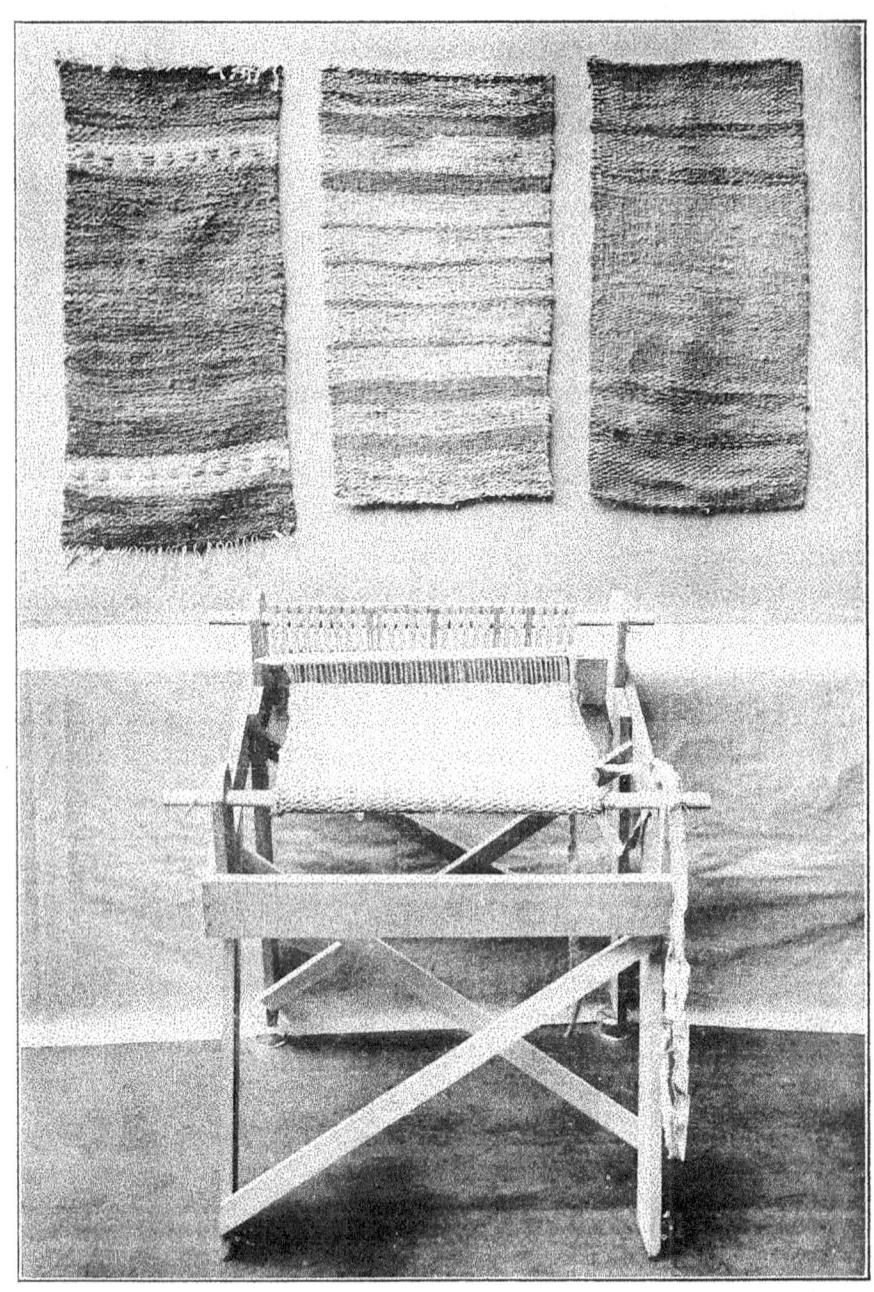

Loom and Rugs. Grade IV.

Assist with wood work for bungalow; cutting shingles and shingling roof.

Make wooden candlesticks and waste-paper baskets. Build and furnish a toy apartment.

Stain articles made by lower grades.

Wood Work. Grades IV and V.

GRADE V

MATERIALS: CLAY, PLASTER, CONCRETE, GLASS, TEXTILES, AND WOOD

Clay.

The pottery industry in the United States; its extent, general location, main pottery centers; workers, wages, factory conditions.

Brief historical sketch of development of industry in this country.

Some typical American wares. The best known foreign wares. Story of Palissy. Longfellow's poem, "Ceramos." Van Dyke's "A Handful of Clay."

Oriental pottery. Visit collection of Chinese porcelains in Metropolitan Museum.

Glazes: their composition, preparation, and coloring.

Shaping clay by lining plaster mold and by casting.

Mosaics: origin, uses, setting. Visit Cathedral of St. John to study mosaics there.

Art modeling: animal forms in the round, birds on tiles, slightly modeled.

Plaster of Paris.

What it is.

Its preparation and uses in making molds and plastering.

Concrete.

Its composition and uses.

Manipulative Work:

Clay: Make vases and mosaic tiles (encaustic), mix colored clays for tiles, mix glazes.

Plaster: Plaster walls of bungalow; make plaster casts.

Concrete: Mix, set mosaics, pour foundation, hearth, mantelpiece, and window boxes for bungalow. Lay concrete walk to bungalow. Make concrete blocks, and build with them. Make fern dishes.

Glass.

Led up to by glaze.

Composition, kinds, uses, methods of shaping; colored glass; Tiffany favrile glass.

Textiles.

Methods of finishing cloths.

Mercerized cotton; artificial silk.

Cloths of mixed materials. Substitutes.

Methods of identifying wool, silk, cotton, and linen in cloth.

Dyes: kinds. Experiments with four textile fibres.

Manipulative Work:

Make some simple tests for four textiles.

Dye samples, and also some of materials used in lower grades.

Wood.

Different cuts of wood. Wood as a building material. House framing.

Edge planing. Planes and similar tools.

Carving as a means of decorating wood.

Manipulative Work:

Assist with wood work for bungalow, making sill, plate, and roof; also molds for concrete work.

Make necktie or hair ribbon racks, picture frames, and book racks. Decorate with simple grooving or carving.

Build frame house (group or individual project).

House Framing. Grade V.

The following is a typical paper written by a pupil of this grade.

VASE MAKING

In factories vases are often made in this manner. A piece of clay is placed on a table, and a boy hammers it out to the desired thickness. Then he hands the layer of clay to a man nearby, who has a mold made of plaster of Paris, which is sometimes in three or four pieces or even more. The man lines each piece of the mold with clay, and then fastens the pieces together. He rubs the seams gently with slip to make the clay stick together. Then he hands it to a boy who carries it to a shelf to dry.

After it is dry, the mold is taken apart and the vase comes out. Many other things besides vases are made in this way; pitchers, bowls, bathtubs, etc.

GRADES VI AND VII

Beginning with the Sixth Grade, and continuing through the Seventh, the boys and girls pursue their work separately, the boys working in the shop, and the girls devoting their time to sewing and cooking. For a detailed statement pertaining to the girls' work see Household Arts. With the general industrial intelligence gained in the first five grades, it is possible to give detailed consideration to the more specific phases of industrial life in modern society. For the purpose of analysis, the industrial work in these grades falls under three heads: materials, processes. and workers. Or, more broadly stated, the first two—materials and processes—comprise the technical phases, and

Concrete Work.   Grade VII

that of the workers comprises the social phases. The technical phases are realized through the construction of various projects, and through shop demonstration, showing the use of various type machines. For this manipulative work there is a seventy-five-minute period each week. The social phases are studied through lectures and discussions, occurring once each week and occupying a thirty-minute period. For a complete statement of this phase of the work, see the closing paragraphs of the course. The industries studied in these grades are lumber and its re-manufacture into various products; metals, including lead. iron. and steel: concrete. including its decorative and structural uses; printing and publishing, including modern printing processes and bookbinding.

GRADE VI

WOOD and METAL industries are studied in this grade.

Wood. Among the projects in wood which have been constructed are simple shelves, clock frames, simple picture frames, and necktie racks. It is in this grade that technical processes in wood are studied in detail. The projects enumerated are the basis for teaching the fundamental processes of squaring, butt joining, boring, nailing, screwing, and gluing, and involve the

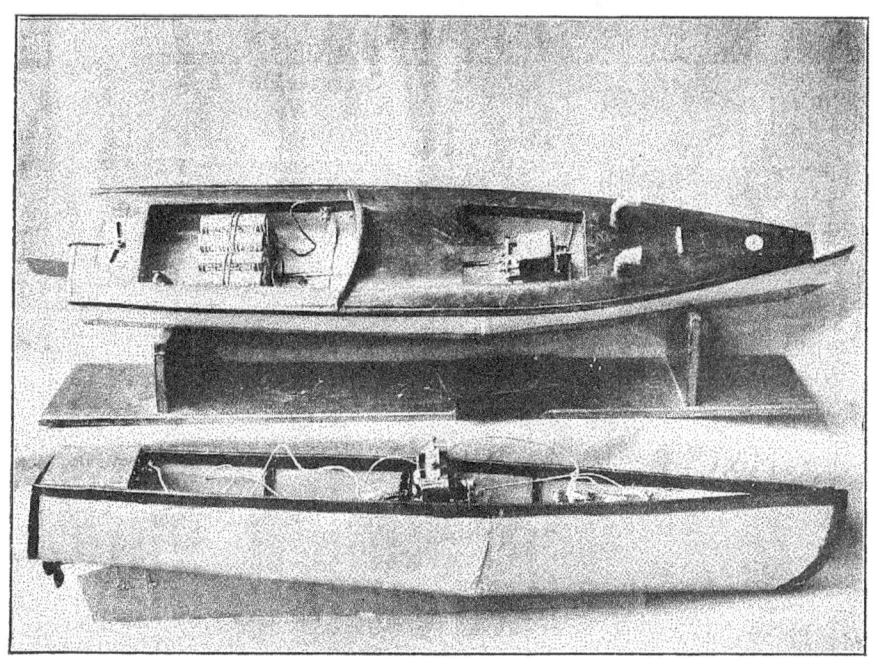

Metal Motor Boats. Grade VII.

use of the common tools such as the plane, the saw, the try-square, the hammer, the bit and brace, and the gauge. The finishing processes are studied in detail and skill is acquired in sandpapering, oiling, rubbing down, waxing, and shellacing. There is direct correlation with the work in fine arts, as the projects constructed in this grade are first designed by the pupils under the direction of the Fine Arts Department.

Metal. Metal work in this grade consists of a study of foundry work, including the casting and finishing processes. A paper weight, cast in lead, is used as a basis for this study. The

Motor Boat Race.   Grade VII.

project involves constructing a pattern in wood and also the casting flask. The casting process includes placing of pattern, tempering and tamping the sand, removing pattern, pouring lead, filing and finishing with emery, and finally the process of electro-plating.

GRADE VII

WOOD, METAL, CONCRETE, PRINTING, and PUBLISHING, are studied in this grade.

Wood. The study of the wood industry occupies but a small portion of the time, but as skill in this material is essential to the other industries studied, it is here included. A simple book rack or shelf is used as a basis for this wood study. The same processes as enumerated under the Sixth Grade course are here studied, but greater emphasis is placed upon accuracy and speed.

Metal. The metal industries are approached through the construction of a motor boat. The boat is made of sheet tin and soft iron. Upon its completion a race is held in the swimming pool. The following processes are involved in the construction of the boat: shaping the strips of soft iron into ribs, shaping the tin, punching holes in the tin and soft iron and riveting the tin to the iron ribs; constructing and soldering the keel to the boat; constructing and mounting the rudder and propeller; and finally mounting the motor and connecting the shaft to the propeller.

As a direct outgrowth of this project, the pupils are led to a study of the elemental physical laws involved, and also to a study of power and its transmission. Under this phase of the work, the steam engine, the gasoline engine, and electric motor, are considered. Models of the various engines are exhibited and studied, and excursions are made to shops where such engines are in operation. Under power transmission are included such devices as shafts, gears, and chains.

Concrete. The construction of a concrete flower-pot is used as a basis for the study of this industry. This project involves the construction of a wooden mold with core, the water-proofing of the mold, the study of the appropriate proportion of sand aggregate and cement, and methods of mixing and pouring this mixture, and lastly methods of curing and coloring the flower-pot.

Printing and Publishing. The study of this industry centers about the problem of binding the written accounts of the industrial work. Such processes as sewing, backing, fastening cover boards, and lettering, are involved. A visit to a publishing house is also included in this study.

RELATED INDUSTRIAL MATERIAL: GRADES VI AND VII

In connection with the actual project work, and at the most appropriate time, the following material is presented. The method of presentation varies with the occasion and the nature of the material, but includes discussions, illustrated lectures, shop and machine demonstrations, and visits to factories and manufacturing establishments.

Industrial Life in New York. This study includes the number and relative distribution of workers in the five groups of human activity; namely, industrial, trade and transportation, domestic and personal service, professional, and agricultural. Copies of Chart 1, which serves as a basis for this study, are placed in the hands of the pupils. A comparative study is made of the relative number in industry with those in other groups in New York City, as well as in other American cities. For this purpose, Chart 2 is used. With this general background, a detailed study is made of the industries of New York City, and the pupils are provided with Chart 3.

Wood Industries. In the first five grades the pupils are given a preliminary industrial insight into the wood industries, and in the Sixth and Seventh grades this material is reviewed and studied more intensively under the following heads: the forest areas of the United States; methods of logging in various parts of the country; the sawmilling process, both primitive and modern; the various cuts of wood; wood structure; wood-working tools and machinery, including circular and platform saws, planers, and mortising-machines. In order to realize the local extent of the wood industries, Chart 4 is used. Aside from these technical phases of the wood industries already enumerated the social phases are also considered. These include the study of industrial accidents, diseases and their prevention, regulation of hours of labor and conditions under which the industry is pursued, and employers' liability acts.

The following outline is one of the series used in the study of the wood industries. A copy is placed in the hands of each pupil, and he becomes familiar with its contents before the discussion.

Wood Industries in New York City

Outline No. 8

In colonial times there were no distinct wood industries. Each man, with the help of his neighbors, built his own barn and house, mended his own tools, and repaired his own furniture.

With the invention of machinery, and the influx of artisans, wood industries developed in the United States. The first saw mill, operated by generated power, was in New England. Carpenters and cabinet makers were expert workmen, and young boys, desiring to learn the trade, would become apprenticed to these men for six or eight years.

As machines were perfected, handwork became less necessary and now the average wood worker is skilled only in tending a machine.

In New York, in the majority of cases, the wood industry is carried on in lofts or deserted tenements, and the ventilation is very poor, causing the workers to breathe a great deal of wood dust.

Workers are also in danger of injury by touching circular and band saws. All such machines can be guarded, but very few are guarded in New York City. There is also some danger from fire.

Children may be employed to do some of the work, and in some cases, children work on toys and pictureframes in their homes.

Directions for Pupils

Study the chart on Wood Industries in New York. Mount it in your booklet with to-day's composition.

Write about any of the industries named in the chart, or on one of these topics:

The dangers to which workers in wood are exposed.

What children can do in wood-working mills.

Metal Industries. A study is here made of the precious as well as the non-precious metals, including the mining and refining processes. Detailed study is made of the iron and steel industry of to-day, and comparisons are made with the industry in former periods of its development. The manufacture of coke, pig iron, various kinds of steel, and also casting and finishing, are included in this study. As in the wood industry, the social phases of this industry are also considered, basing the study upon such topics as, the loss of life in the pursuit of the industry, from both direct and indirect causes; the measures being considered to prevent this enormous loss of life; the means of caring for the dependent families made so through loss of father or brother, and the number and condition of immigrants in the industry. Biographical studies of some of the great inventors are also included.

Concrete. A historic study is made of the cement industries showing the rapid growth of the industry in recent years. The composition, source of raw materials, and the manufacture of cement, as well as the mixtures for various purposes, receive consideration in this grade. The uses of cement, including the various structural and ornamental phases are here included. The dangers to which workmen are subjected in the cement process, as well as the prevention of these dangers, are considered.

HOW WORKERS IN NEW YORK CITY ARE DIVIDED IN OCCUPATION.

■MEN.　▨WOMEN.

INDUSTRIAL.

MEN	WOMEN	TOTAL.
419,594	132,535	552,129

TRADE and TRANSPORTATION

MEN	WOMEN	TOTAL
405,675	65,318	470,993

PROFESSIONAL

MEN	WOMEN	TOTAL
60,853	22,422	83,275

DOMESTIC and PERSONAL SERVICE

MEN	WOMEN	TOTAL
206,215	146,722	352,937

AGRICULTURAL

MEN	WOMEN	TOTAL
10,134	440	10,574

Chart 1.

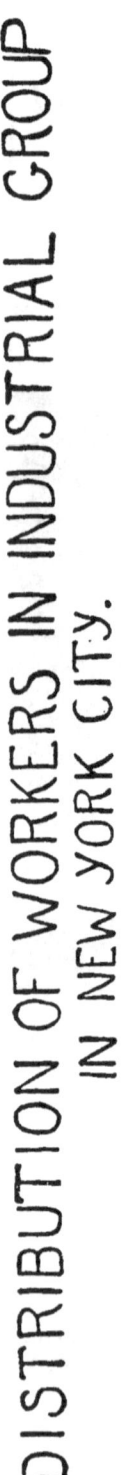

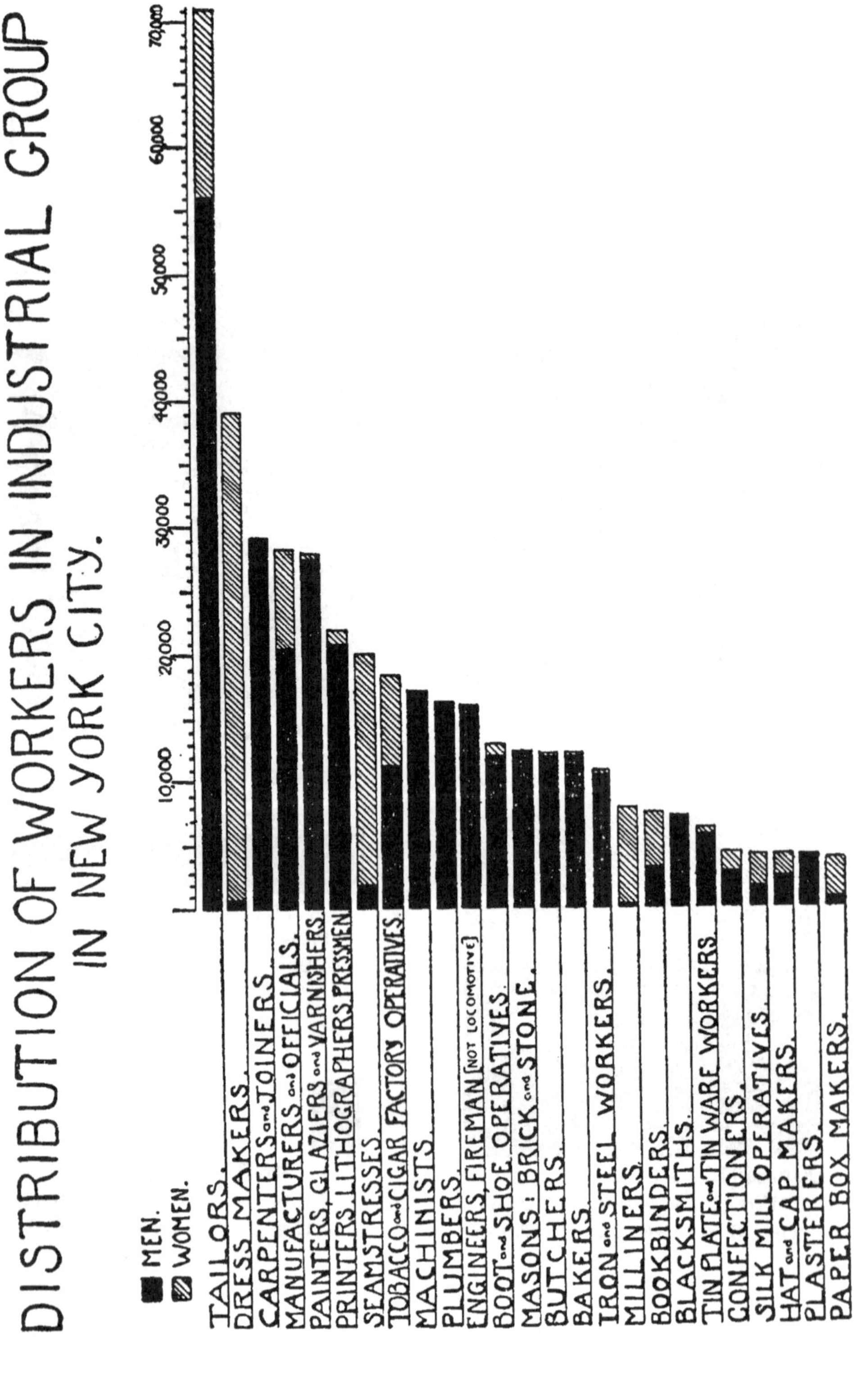
DISTRIBUTION OF WORKERS IN INDUSTRIAL GROUP
IN NEW YORK CITY.
MEN.
WOMEN.
10,000
20,000
30,000
40,000
50,000
60,000
70,000
TAILORS.
DRESS MAKERS.
CARPENTERS and JOINERS.
MANUFACTURERS and OFFICIALS.
PAINTERS, GLAZIERS and VARNISHERS.
PRINTERS, LITHOGRAPHERS, PRESSMEN.
SEAMSTRESSES.
TOBACCO and CIGAR FACTORY OPERATIVES.
MACHINISTS.
PLUMBERS.
ENGINEERS, FIREMAN (NOT LOCOMOTIVE)
BOOT and SHOE OPERATIVES.
MASONS: BRICK and STONE.
BUTCHERS.
BAKERS.
IRON and STEEL WORKERS.
MILLINERS.
BOOKBINDERS.
BLACKSMITHS.
TIN PLATE and TIN WARE WORKERS.
CONFECTIONERS.
SILK MILL OPERATIVES.
HAT and CAP MAKERS.
PLASTERERS.
PAPER BOX MAKERS.

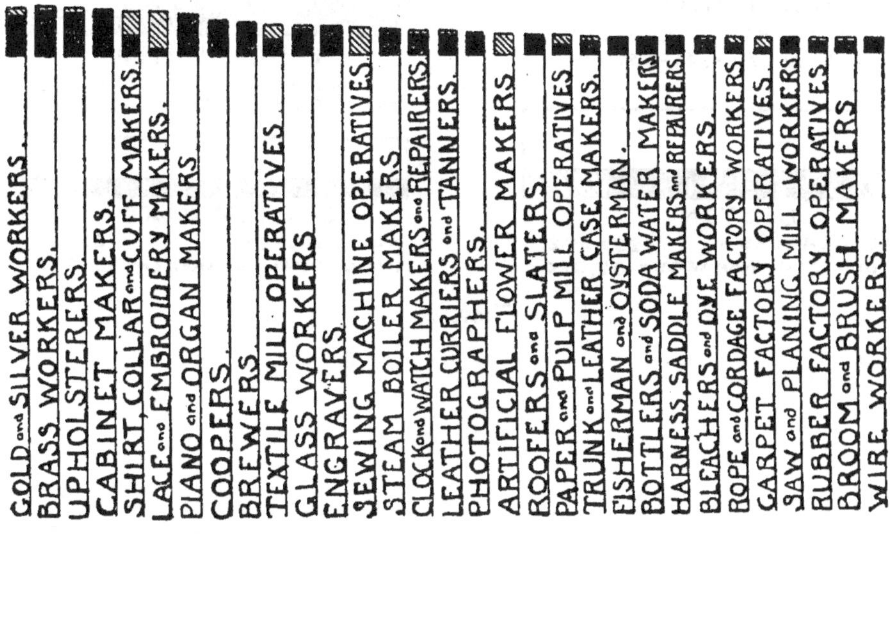

Chart 3.

GOLD and SILVER WORKERS.
BRASS WORKERS.
UPHOLSTERERS.
CABINET MAKERS.
SHIRT, COLLAR and CUFF MAKERS.
LACE and EMBROIDERY MAKERS.
PIANO and ORGAN MAKERS.
COOPERS.
BREWERS.
TEXTILE MILL OPERATIVES.
GLASS WORKERS.
ENGRAVERS.
SEWING MACHINE OPERATIVES.
STEAM BOILER MAKERS.
CLOCK and WATCH MAKERS and REPAIRERS.
LEATHER CURRIERS and TANNERS.
PHOTOGRAPHERS.
ARTIFICIAL FLOWER MAKERS.
ROOFERS and SLATERS.
PAPER and PULP MILL OPERATIVES.
TRUNK and LEATHER CASE MAKERS.
FISHERMAN and OYSTERMAN.
BOTTLERS and SODA WATER MAKERS.
HARNESS, SADDLE MAKERS and REPAIRERS.
BLEACHERS and DYE WORKERS.
ROPE and CORDAGE FACTORY WORKERS.
CARPET FACTORY OPERATIVES.
SAW and PLANING MILL WORKERS.
RUBBER FACTORY OPERATIVES.
BROOM and BRUSH MAKERS.
WIRE WORKERS.

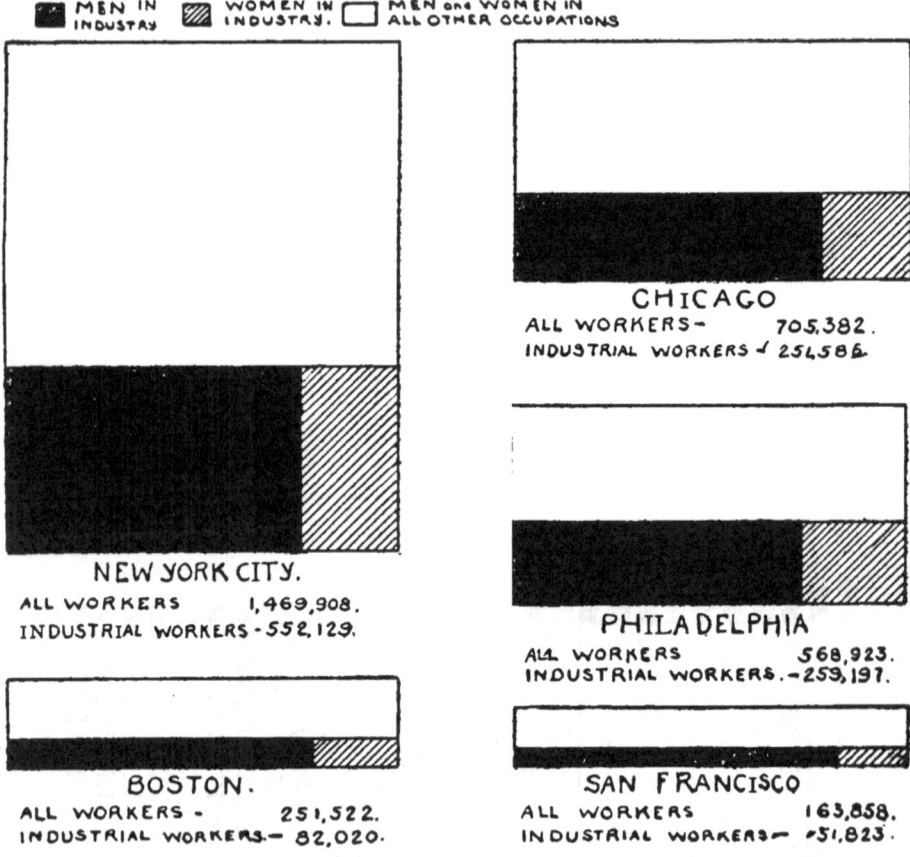

COMPARISON OF NUMBER OF WORKERS IN
INDUSTRIAL GROUP WITH NUMBER OF
WORKERS IN ALL GROUPS. - FIVE CITIES.

MEN IN INDUSTRY   WOMEN IN INDUSTRY.   MEN and WOMEN IN ALL OTHER OCCUPATIONS

CHICAGO
ALL WORKERS -   705,382.
INDUSTRIAL WORKERS ✔ 256,586.

NEW YORK CITY.
ALL WORKERS   1,469,908.
INDUSTRIAL WORKERS - 552,129.

PHILADELPHIA
ALL WORKERS   568,923.
INDUSTRIAL WORKERS. - 253,197.

BOSTON.
ALL WORKERS -   251,522.
INDUSTRIAL WORKERS. - 82,020.

SAN FRANCISCO
ALL WORKERS   163,858.
INDUSTRIAL WORKERS ― ✔51,823.

Chart 2.

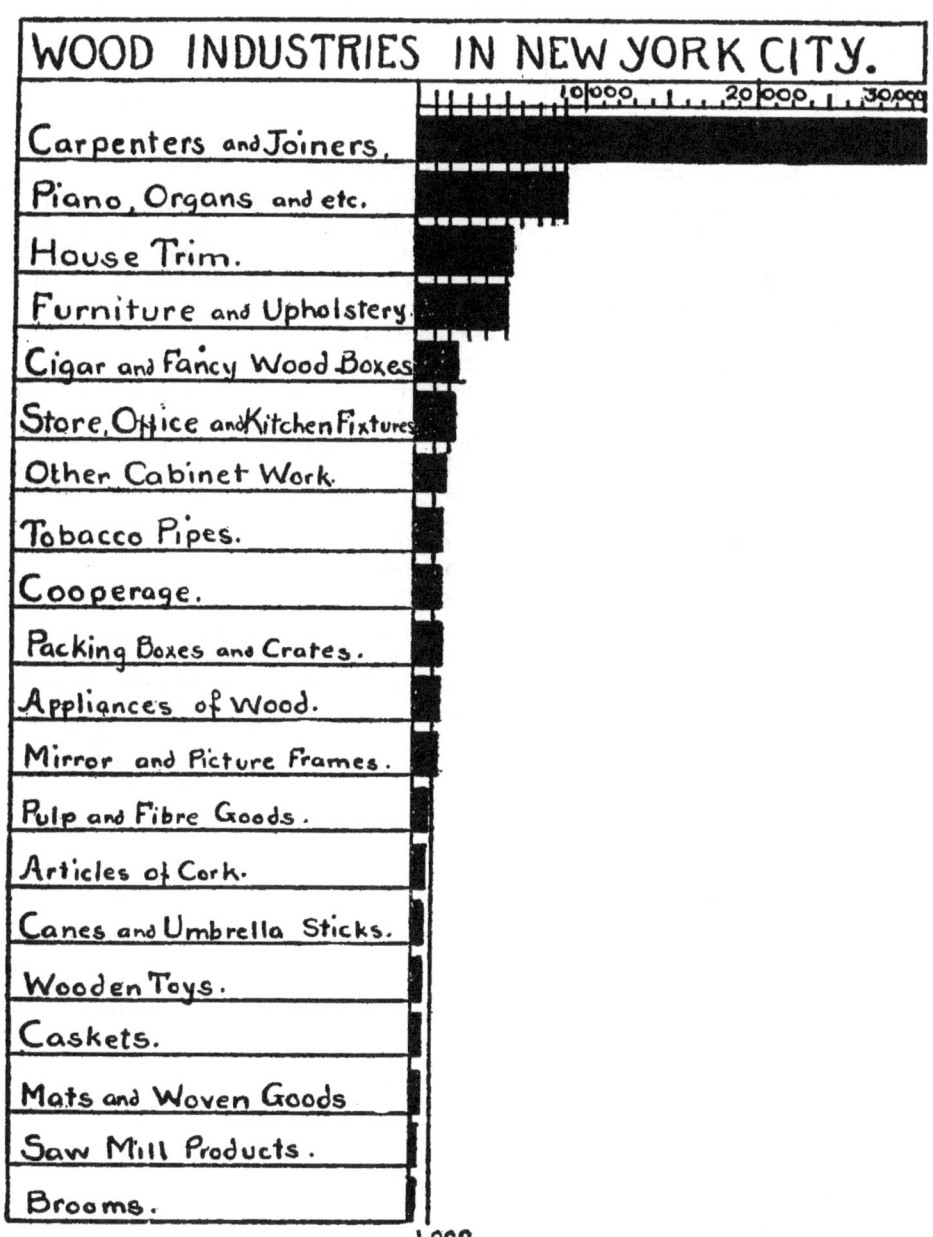

WOOD INDUSTRIES IN NEW YORK CITY.

| | 10,000 | 20,000 | 30,000 |

Carpenters and Joiners,
Piano, Organs and etc.
House Trim.
Furniture and Upholstery.
Cigar and Fancy Wood Boxes
Store, Office and Kitchen Fixtures
Other Cabinet Work.
Tobacco Pipes.
Cooperage.
Packing Boxes and Crates.
Appliances of Wood.
Mirror and Picture Frames.
Pulp and Fibre Goods.
Articles of Cork.
Canes and Umbrella Sticks.
Wooden Toys.
Caskets.
Mats and Woven Goods
Saw Mill Products.
Brooms.

1,000

Chart 4.

CHART SHOWING THE CONSTRUCTIVE WORK IN

INDUSTRY OR INDUSTRIAL MATERIAL	GRADE I	GRADE II	GRADE III
CLAY	Toy dishes, paper weights, trays, marbles. Orange, grapefruit, tangerine, lemon.	Fern dishes, tiles. Indian bowls, beads. Jack-o-lantern. Snow man, Indian figures. Apple, pear, pumpkin.	Bricks for house. Tiles for fireplace. Flower pots, art tiles. Relief of rosette or flower form.
TEXTILES	Rug, curtains, etc., for doll house on cardboard looms. Doll hammock on wooden frame loom. Reed work basket.	Indian suit, head-dress and mocca-sins, shoe-bags, bookmark, mat, rugs for Indian village. Print cloth. Indian basket. Indian loom.	Wool—wash, card, spin, etc. Penwiper, needle-book. Plain, mixed, striped and plaid cloths.
WOOD	Looms, doll furniture, hammock, stands, farmhouses, Eskimo sheds, etc.	Ring toss game, beanbag board. Tile mold.	Brick molds. Continuous warp looms. Framework of house—cutting flooring and shingles.
PAPER AND PRINTING	Booklets, box, paper the doll house.	Booklets.	Box with fitted cover. Booklets.
CONCRETE			
METAL			
GROUP PROJECTS	Farm scene. Eskimo village.	Indian village. Robinson Crusoe Pueblo.	Brick house.

ONNECTION WITH THE VARIOUS INDUSTRIES

GRADE IV	GRADE V	GRADE VI	GRADE VI
erra cotta for house. lates, paper weights, candlesticks. omato, beets, carrots, in round and in relief.	Vases—Mosaics. Birds in relief, animal in round.		
eave diagonal and figured cloths, sofa pillows or rug. ugs, curtains, pillows, etc., for apartment furnishings. eave class rug on Colonial loom.	Experiments in testing and dyeing wool cotton silk linen.		
aste-paper basket. ramework of house— nailing floor boards and shingles. uild and make furniture for apartment.	Necktie or hair ribbon rack. Book rack. House framing. Molds for Mosaics. Molds—for foundation of brick house and hearth.	Shelf, clock frame, picture frame and necktie rack.	Book rack, shelf, etc.
aper apartment. encil and print papers.			Binding a booklet, w related wc
	Set Mosaics. Pour foundation and hearth for brick house. Make concrete blocks and build with them.	.	Concrete flo pot.
		Foundry work. Casting lead paper weight.	
ick house. artment.	Brick house. Frame house.		

HOUSEHOLD ARTS

The work in Industrial Arts for the first five grades is pre-scribed for both boys and girls, but at the beginning of the Sixth Grade a differentiation is made, the boys continuing in the field of industry, while the girls begin the study of some of the more practical problems of their subsequent life-work.

SIXTH GRADE

The work of the Sixth Grade is an elementary course in sew-ing, together with some study of materials and a brief survey of the conditions underlying the garment-making industries of this city. One hour each week for the year is the time assign-ment.

During the year the elementary stitches are taught in the process of making various articles. Running, backstitching, overhanding, hemming, stocking darning, and simple embroidery are used on such articles as cooking or sewing aprons, bags, traveling cases, and desk-sets. The designs for the desk-sets are made by the girls in their art class, then transferred to the linen and embroidered. Darning is first taught on stockinet, then stockings are brought from home and darned in the class.

Considerable attention is given to the technique of sewing, for most of the girls have never worn a thimble, many have never held a needle, and none of them can cut in a straight line. Until the proper use of these tools becomes an unconscious habit, sewing is hard work, and not much progress can be made in doing a piece of work well and easily.

Besides the construction work in sewing, some knowledge of other subjects closely allied to it is gained, e.g., a study of the materials used and a feeling of responsibility for the good taste displayed in choosing them. Likewise, some practice in the eco-nomic buying and cutting of material is gained as each girl plans, cuts, and makes each article herself.

Some phases of the social and industrial problems connected with the work and closely related to the study of New York City are taken up, such as the garment-making industry, the number of people employed in it in the city, conditions under which they work, what is being done to improve these conditions, child labor laws, factory inspection, and the Consumers' League.

The work is made as practical as possible, and we hope that such interest will be aroused that the girls will desire a further knowledge of the subject. This they may get in the High School, where a further study of the subject is open to them in the Second, Fourth, and Fifth years. These courses include garment-making, simple millinery, dressmaking, and embroidery. They give a more comprehensive idea of textile and social problems and the responsibility which rests on the consumer. They deal more with the cost of clothes, and the planning of personal and household allowances.

SEVENTH GRADE

The work of the Seventh Grade is cooking and some of its allied problems, such as the manufacture of staple foodstuffs, elements of sanitation, food inspection, and the pure food laws. The time assignment is one and a quarter hours each week.

A few girls have helped at home or watched the cook, but the majority know nothing of housekeeping, and owing to the development of apartment hotels in the city some have never even been in a kitchen. Everything is to be learned, the names and uses of utensils, how to light the gas range, different methods of cooking and cleaning, and sometimes how to strike a match.

The aim of the seventh year course is, then, a practical one—to give the girls experience in household activities, skill in manipulation, and by actual cooking to teach them some essentials in the successful management of a home.

Of course many of these children may never need to cook, and for them the value of such practical work is only secondary. Each one, however, is directly affected by general living conditions, since health and proper food are vital to us all. An attempt is made, therefore, to interest the children in the food conditions surrounding us in a great city, and to make them ready to coöperate intelligently in sanitary regulations.

In direct cooking lessons each child prepares the dish individually, while class discussion develops a study of the foodstuffs, their cost, production or manufacture, how affected by heat, and in a simple way their composition and use in the body. For example, in the chop lesson a study is made of meat. The children recall from their geography and history how cattle are raised on the western ranches and speak of the great Chicago packing houses. Then they make a list of causes for the cost of beef, including the wages of cowboys and packers, transformation of ranches into the more profitable farms in certain states, control by trusts, unnecessary number of city markets, and the expense of transportation. This latter point interests them especially, as the geography class studies the growth of commercial centers and the cost of freightage by boat and railroad. The girls then draw diagrams of cuts of meat, discuss tests for good marketing, examine the structure of muscles, and watch the albumen whiten in cooking.

The pupils keep note-books in which they write an original summary of each lesson. These are used in the English class as material for written home work and are then reviewed by the teacher of domestic science. Insistence is made on clear, coherent answers, and frequently the class conducts its own reviews, criticising a recitation not only for the facts presented, but also for the manner of presenting them.

In order that the girls may intelligently control the helpful forces of nature, the simple and most useful facts in chemistry and physics are presented as the need arises. They are taught the principles of expansion and contraction through the boiling of water or the freezing of ice cream, the action of alkalis in cleaning, the readiness of acids to combine with metals as seen on tarnished knives, and the formation of gas found in various leavening agents.

No distinct cleaning lesson is given in the Seventh Grade, but naturally emphasis falls on ideals of sanitation, neatness, ease and daintiness in work, while every girl is responsible for the order and cleanliness of her own utensils.

Helpfulness at home is encouraged, and school methods are related to home conditions as closely as equipment and convenience permit. The girls are taught to rely on themselves, and frequently tell with pride how they cooked some dish at home when "the cook was out."

At the end of the school year, the class gives to four or six teachers a luncheon which is prepared during the regular lesson period, and served after school at one o'clock. The children write the invitations, plan a balanced menu, make the marketing list, and arrange the table decorations. Half the class cook the food, while the others prepare the dining room. If the size of the class permits, each girl has the coveted honor of serving some dish, and after the lunch all the children delightedly usher the guests into the kitchen to show how neat they have kept the room. The following is an outline of the course.

1. Baked apples
2. Apple sauce—dish-washing
3. Cooking cereal
4. Review cereal—mold it with fruit
5. Cornstarch mold
6. Starch experiments—salted almonds
7. Study of egg—scrambling egg
8. Soft custard
9. Meat cuts—pan broiled chops
10. Beef tea—study of meat
11. Holiday lesson—candy
12. Creamed potatoes
13. Cream soup—study of milk
14. Popovers
15. Griddle cakes (sour milk)
16. Muffins—study of flour
17. Gingerbread
18. Baking powder biscuit
19. Light omelet
20. Sponge cake
21. Waldorf salad (boiled dressing)
22. Lemon jelly
23. Orange charlotte
24. Yeast experiments
25. Bread
26. Raised biscuits
27. Visit bakery
28. Butter cake
29. Plan luncheon
30. Luncheon to teachers
31. Review
32. Ice cream

We believe the love of the beautiful to be as instinctive as any emotion, "that art is an expression of energy in terms of beauty" (A. W. Dow), "an artist one who gives form to a beautiful conception" (C. H. Caffin), and that "a child has the right to five inheritances—religious, literary, scientific, aesthetic, and institutional" (N. M. Butler). Consequently, the aim of art in the curriculum is to aid in the general rounding out of the child's character by enriching and making useful the aesthetic side of his nature. This may be done through the development of appreciation by association with works of art in the original, lantern slides, and pictures; of critical judgment through comparison of good and poor work in class criticism; and of expression by problems in line, in light and dark, and in color.

The subjects for study are drawn from the child's immediate interests, that is, from other studies such as industrial art, geography, history, and reading, as well as from holiday seasons, and from home life. The method is adapted to the child's development; and the materials are water color, crayon, cut paper, stencil wood-block, mosaic, clay, brush, charcoal, or pencil, as best suits the case, the object always being to help the child to help himself.

In the first three grades the play spirit predominates—the mere joy of trying to make things, and to make them beautiful as well as useful. The subjects are taken from things which are a part of the child's life and which can be quickly accomplished, the aim being to keep the naïve quality of childhood

Grade II. Illustration. Colored Cut Paper (Class Problem).

and to give only the means of expression which will make the pupil's work as original, rhythmic, and delightful as primitive art.

The utilitarian spirit develops later, and with it the desire to " work for work's sake," and also for the sake of the results to be obtained. To meet this spirit, in the Fourth, Fifth, and Sixth grades more elaborate problems are given which are to be utilized in household and industrial arts, or in some other branch of study. Between these longer and harder problems, quicker, freer problems are given for the relaxation that child nature demands. The freehand drawing with the brush, of flowers, animals, and figures, which is done in all six grades, has been a most satisfactory feature of the work, and productive of both freedom and skill.

Each grade has talks upon pictures and works of art appropriate to the age of the children and the subjects studied. Every room is provided with a permanent art frame in which art subjects are always on exhibition and for which the two lower grades make pictures, from cut paper, of some subject in which they are interested. This is a final problem and the result of united class effort.

The class work for 1912-13 is along the following lines:

FIRST GRADE

Rhythm and color differences of hue, being art instincts which are unquestionably developed early in child life, are the art principles upon which most of the First Grade work is based, and the fact is developed that to make things show some must be dark and some light.

In repeating single units to form groups some child is certain to emphasize one unit of the group, leading quite naturally from the principle of rhythm to subordination, which is the plan of both home and school life, and from which the subject matter of this grade is taken. Rhythmic borders are made for clay bowls by arranging seeds on the clay and pressing them in. When dry, a pattern remains in intaglio. These arrangements may be further developed by making seed forms with simple brush strokes on paper, from which more elaborate things, such as flowers, animals, and people in action, are developed and used in illustrations for reading books. Designs are also made for these books from little forms that the children cut from

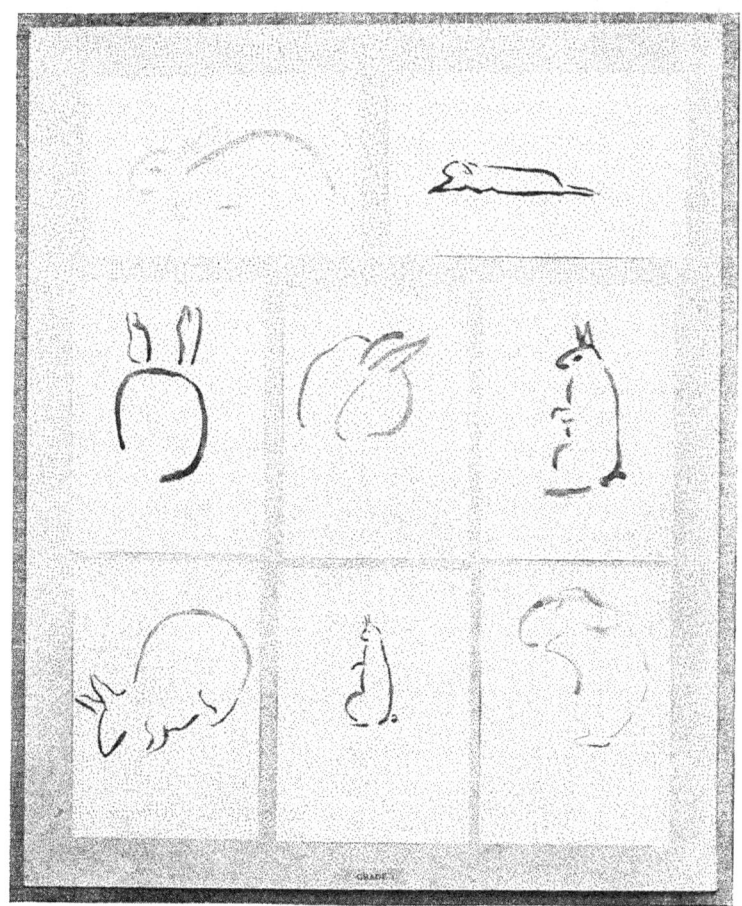

Grade I. Action. Brush Drawing

colored paper and arrange in rhythmic patterns. Again, on the first of May, baskets are cut and pasted on a cover, and these are filled with flowers of the children's own choice and cutting. Another rhythmic pattern is a wallpaper for a room that the children fit out.

The simpler brush stroke objects are enlarged as the power grows to make larger objects in outline and wash drawings.

The pumpkin seed becomes a pumpkin, and at Hallowe'en a group of Jack-o-lanterns is made from cut paper. In the difference between a jolly and a sober Jack-o-lantern comes the first lesson in facial expression. The orange family will be cut from colored paper and arranged on plates cut by the children. Later, it will be followed to its native land and painted

Grade I. Rhythm   Brush Drawing in Color.

growing on the branch. The Christmas trees used in designs for Christmas cards will be made to grow in groups on their native heath of snow. "Raggylug," the "Country and City Mouse," squirrels, and other animals, are carried through a succession of antics to a final class composition in cut paper for the art frame of this grade.

The imitative faculty, another instinct strongly developed in little children, is allowed full sway in the representation of realistic forms. Form being of a most symbolic character in the expression of a first grade child, the teacher often paints with the children in these exercises, and the originality of the child naturally asserts itself, producing some delightful variations of the original subject.

In order to meet the childish love for coloring pictures, hectographed copies of good and appropriate subjects are sometimes given to the children at holiday seasons, such as a holly branch at Christmas time, or a butterfly for Easter.

The materials most used are water colors, clay, and colored crayons.

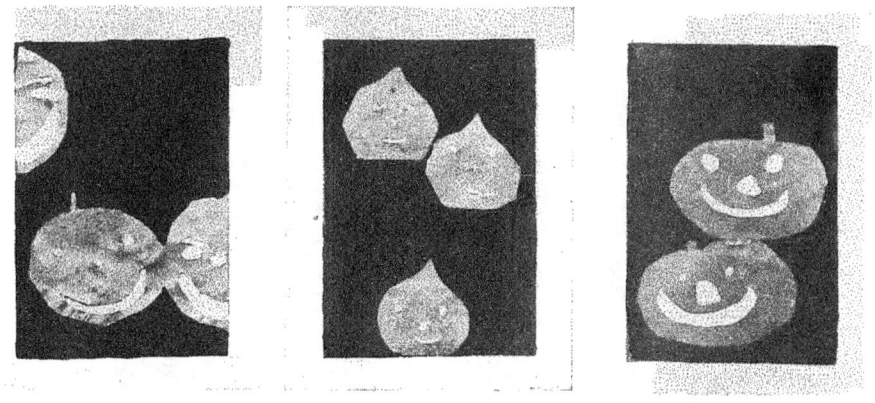

Grade I. Hallowe'en Night. An Arrangement in Cut Paper.

SECOND GRADE

In the Second Grade, the problems are of much the same character as in the First Grade, differing more in subject matter and in variety of shapes and arrangement than in art principles. Color is emphasized here, as in the earlier grade. Shepherd life, Indian life, early days in Manhattan, and the industries these subjects include, as well as conditions immediately surrounding the children, form the source of subject matter.

The rhythmic borders are arrangements of objects chosen by the child (animals made by brush strokes, or objects cut from colored paper), and used for patterns on the books they make, or for portfolios for school work, and Christmas cards. Garden-making is used in the spring as a subject for a portfolio cover. Each child cuts from colored paper the particular

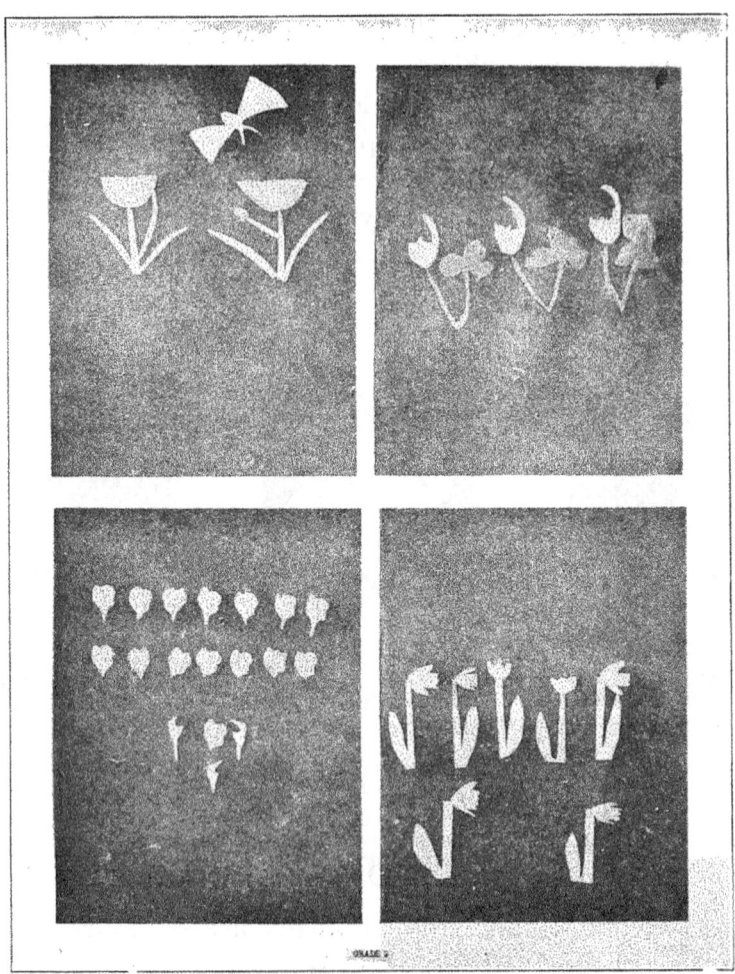

Grade II.   Gardens.   Colored Cut Paper.

kinds of flowers desired for his garden, and pastes them on the dark brown cover as he would plant them in the newly turned earth. The result of this is most satisfactory.

In the fall, apple and pear shapes are studied on the branch, and the drawing is used as a pattern for a tile made in the industrial art work. Later, the pears and apples found in city groceries are painted, and also cut from colored paper and arranged in a basket of the child's design and decoration at Thanksgiving time.

One division of this grade makes a frieze of cut paper for the class-room wall, representing an Indian village, while the other division makes a pueblo for the class-room frame. Other

Grade II. Baskets of Fruit. Arrangement in Colored Cut Paper.

subjects studied this year are the following: a straight line rug pattern for the weaving; a snowman in a winter landscape; the difference between sunny and gray days; trees in summer and autumn; and animals belonging to shepherd life.

Some holiday subjects are a turkey painted at Thanksgiving time; Denslow's "Santa Claus," at the Christmas season; and, for Easter, Okio's "Family of Chickens."

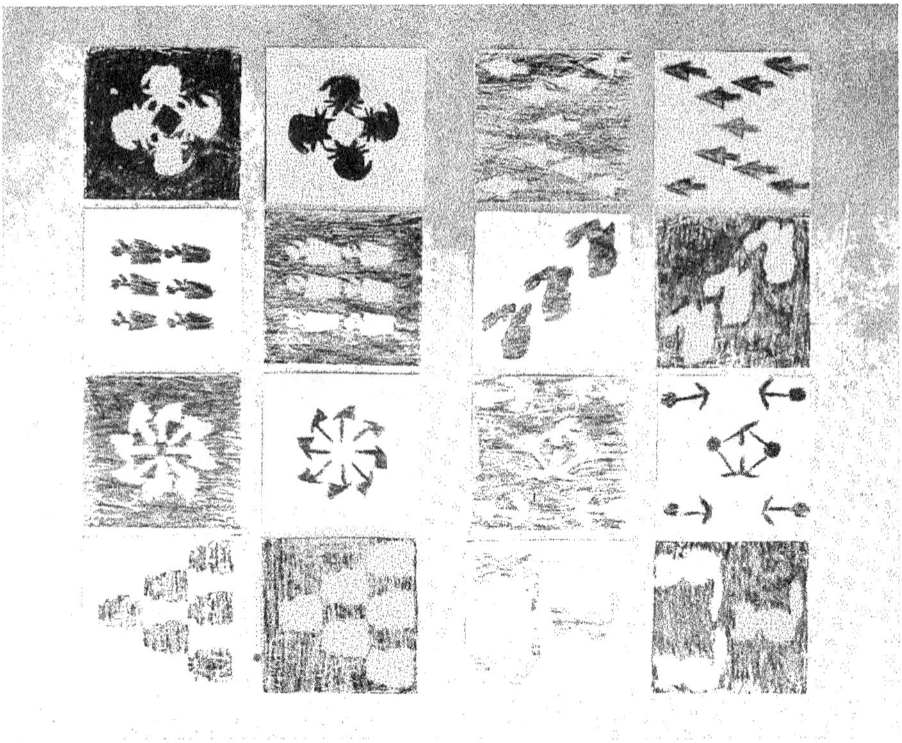

Grade III. Designs for Tiles. Blue and White Crayola.

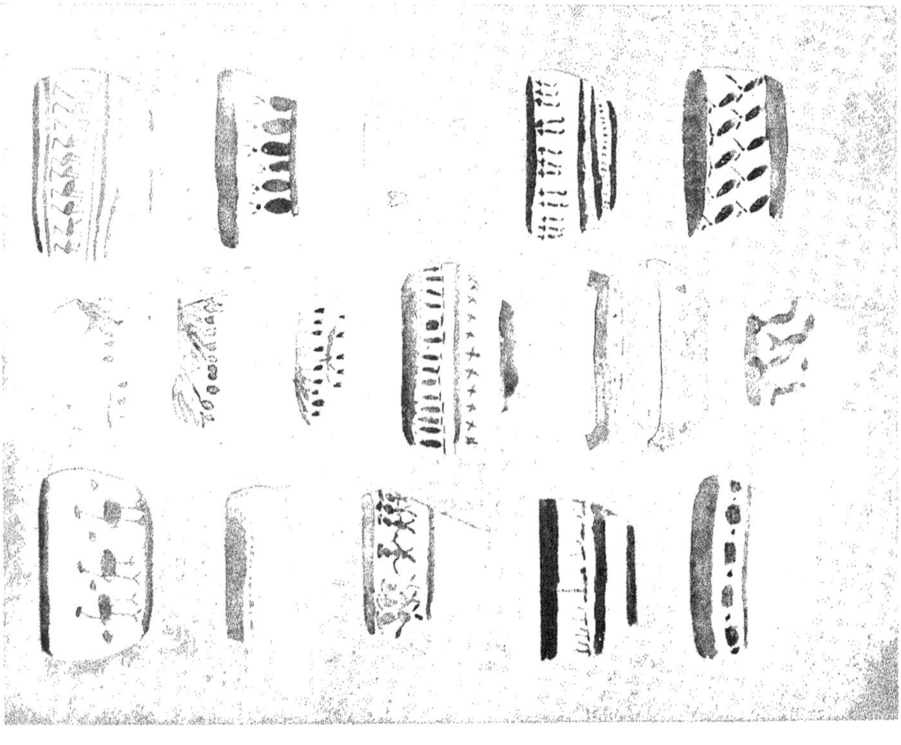

Grade II. Designs for Bowls. Brush Drawing in Color.

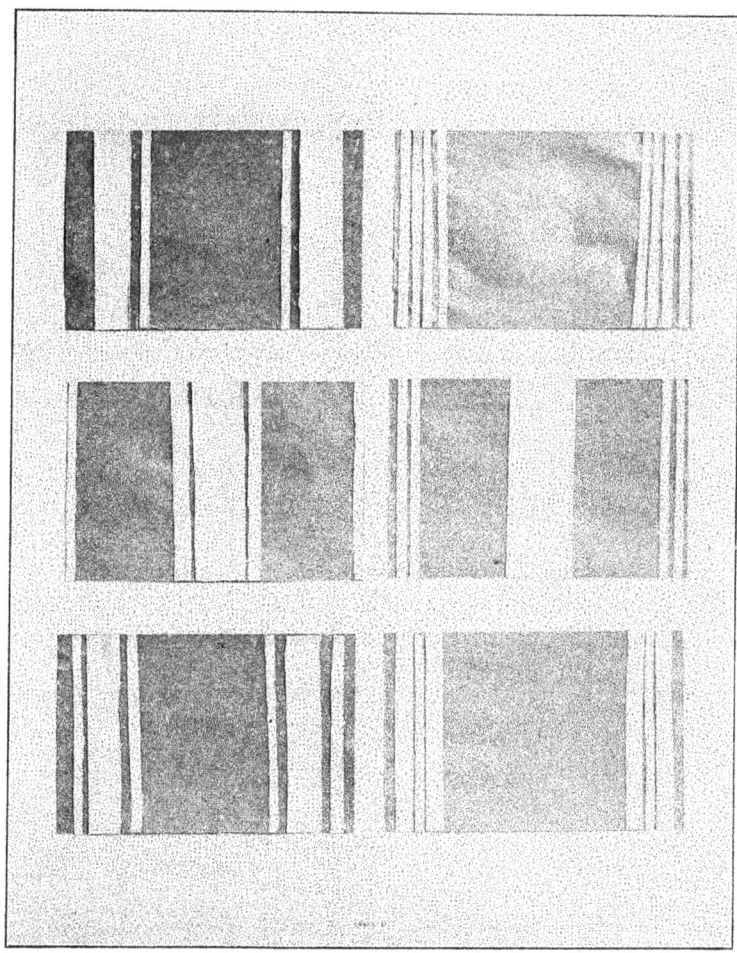

Grade II. Designs for Rugs. Colored Cut Paper.

THIRD GRADE

In the Third Grade the subject matter is expressed with more art values. A beginning is made in calling the various means of expression by their names. Definite problems are given in the choice of line arrangements, in two or three values of dark-and-light, and in a rounding-up of elementary color combinations. Paper cutting is here exchanged for outline drawing, and only used as a means of procuring an outline in repeating patterns. Water color is most used, and colored crayon and charcoal as needed.

Emphasis is put upon the child's own experience. The rhyth-

mic patterns are the child's choice in subject, design, and arrangement. A centered pattern is made for a tile to be executed in blue and white underglaze in the industrial art class, using a unit which represents the thing the child liked best during the summer vacation. A border pattern is made for the cover of a book of poems. Dutch life and masterpieces are studied in connection with the history and customs of Holland and early New York.

Children in action are a special study in the Third Grade. Brush-stroke girls and boys sliding and skating are painted during the winter season in either local or Dutch landscapes. in bright, gray or stormy weather; likewise the actions of the Fire Department are represented in relation to the study of New York City. The brush-stroke people are later enlarged to drawings in outline or colored wash, either from schoolmates

Grades II and III. Roof School. "Moonlight on Roof." Subordination in Dark and Light.

or from models.   Flowers both wild and cultivated are painted in connection with nature-study.   The cow in a spring land-scape illustrates the source of the pure milk supply.

At Christmas time these children write a Christmas verse for their parents in their best handwriting, for which they make a cover decorated with Christmas trees.   The Easter les-son is a lily painted from a subject, or a hectographed model filled in with color.

FOURTH GRADE

The children of this grade show a marked desire and ability for a more grown-up point of view, and this is made a turning point in elementary art.   Emphasis is put upon the child's doing well what he desires to express, and learning the means good artists have used.   Much more time is taken to develop some of the problems, which are made definite ones in line spacing of rhythm and subordination; dark-and-light massing of two or three values, and the effect of tone; color, the theory and color differences of hue, dark-and-light, and intensity.   These are worked out as the application demands their use, and the response of the grade to this method is most encouraging.

One problem is a design for a plate, with both center and border, the kind of pattern and the unit used being the child's choice and carefully adapted to the spaces already prepared in the plate each child has made.   In connection with this a trip is taken to the Metropolitan Museum to see the plates there, and collections of Persian, Spanish, Italian, Japanese, and mod-ern plates in other museums are studied from photographs. Another interesting industrial problem is a rug pattern made for weaving, in which the choice of spaces and colors is worked out as an art problem.

Vegetables from the garden planted in the spring are sub-jects of study in line spacing and color, while water-color draw-ings are made at Christmas and Easter of the flowers in season. Printing is taken up in connection with a cover for a magazine produced by the children; New York streets are studied in comparison with country roads; and a lecture on the Parthenon. given by the head of the Fine Arts Department at Teachers College in connection with the study of Greek art and history. is an event in the year's work.

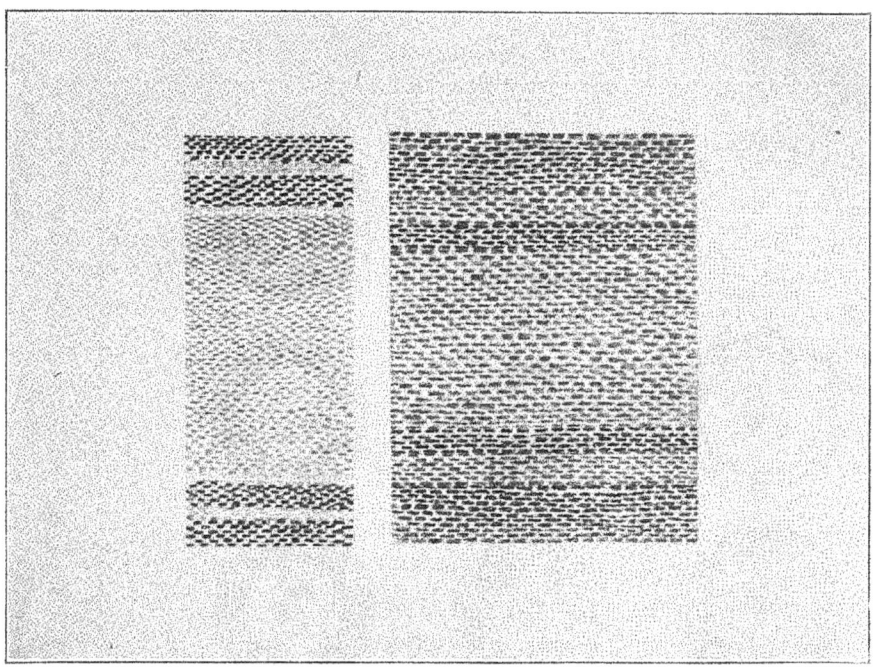

Grade IV. Designs for Rugs. Three Colors. Three Values. Crayola.

Grade IV. Flower Arrangement. Brush Drawing in Color.

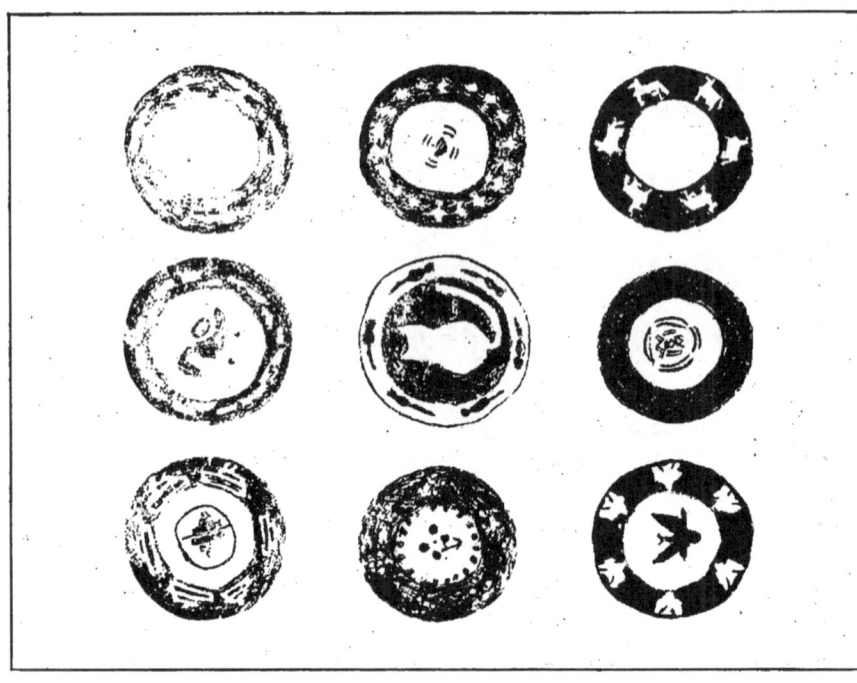

Grade IV.   Designs for Plates.   Blue in Two Values, Crayola.

Grade IV.   Portfolio Covers.   Three Values, Water Color Drawing.

FIFTH GRADE

The principal problems of this grade are designs for useful articles which will be materialized in industrial art work. Rhythm and subordination of line are reviewed and applied in a design for a vase shape. Symmetrical spacing is studied in a centered design for a square mosaic, to be carried out in

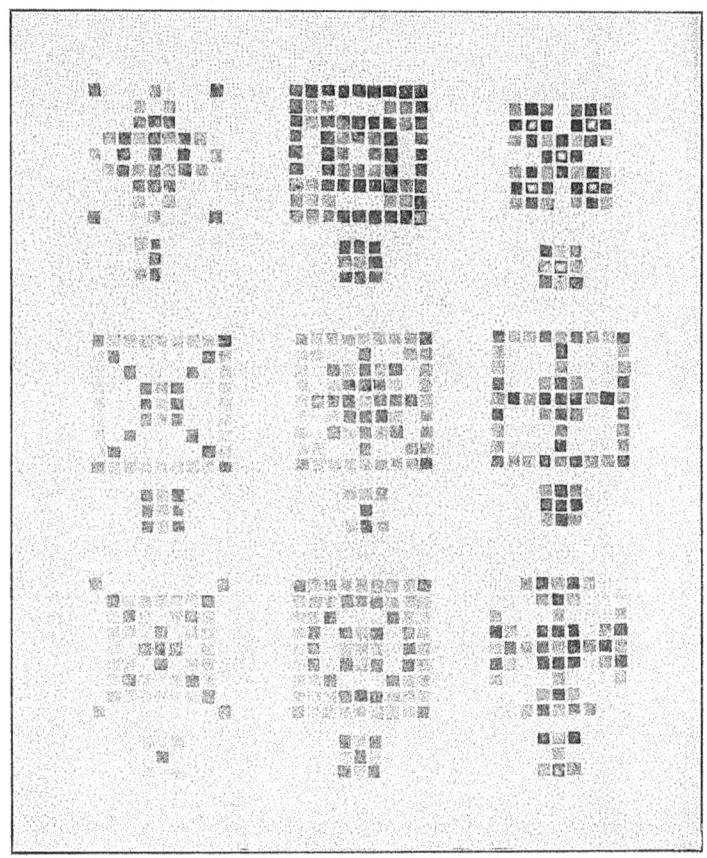

Grade V. Design for Mosaic. Colored Cut Paper.

paper of three values and of three or four hues. The best of these designs are chosen to be made in the industrial art class of pottery and used to decorate the roof school, being a weather proof material. The same design is re-adapted to an oblong rug border pattern carried out in colored crayon upon toned paper. The color problem being, tone in three hues, four values, and the developed necessity of a difference in intensity.

Our museums, with their good illustrations in pottery, rugs, and mosaics, and a trip to St. John's Cathedral to see mosaics, are points in the study of New York City; while the mosaics of St. Mark's in Venice, the Taj Mahal in India, Ravenna, Siena, Rome, and Florence, are studied in comparison. Venice

Grade V. Action. Brush Drawing in Black.

is studied by means of photographs and lantern slides in its connection with the Orient and the resulting influence upon the art of Europe, and the great Gothic cathedrals and their sculptures, in connection with mediaeval history. In connection with nature-study, birds form a subject of special attention, first as to line harmony, and later in dark-and-light, and color composition. These drawings are made entirely with the brush. Brush drawings in color are also made of flowers in season.

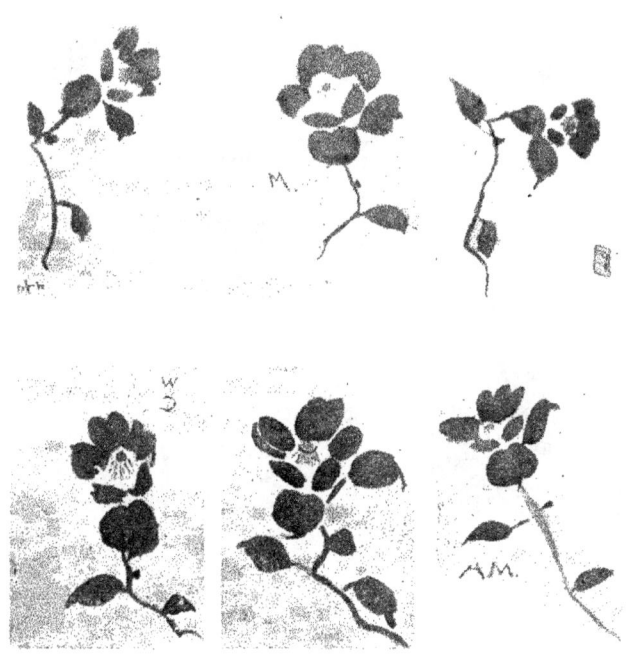

Grade V. Flower Arrangements. Brush Drawing in Color

SIXTH GRADE

The Sixth Grade, which is the last year of the first half of a child's school life, is made a rounding-up place for art principles from an elementary point of view. The principles of good line spacing, dark-and-light massing, and five differences in hue, dark-and-light, and intense coloring, are brought into the problems of the year.

The keynote of the historical study in this grade being modern, the art work follows this lead in the selection of subject matter. In connection with the study of New York City, some of the principal works of art of this city are taken up, also certain phases of art in the colonial period, and some of the great examples of the Renaissance are used as a background for modern art. Fine opportunity for study of perspective, as

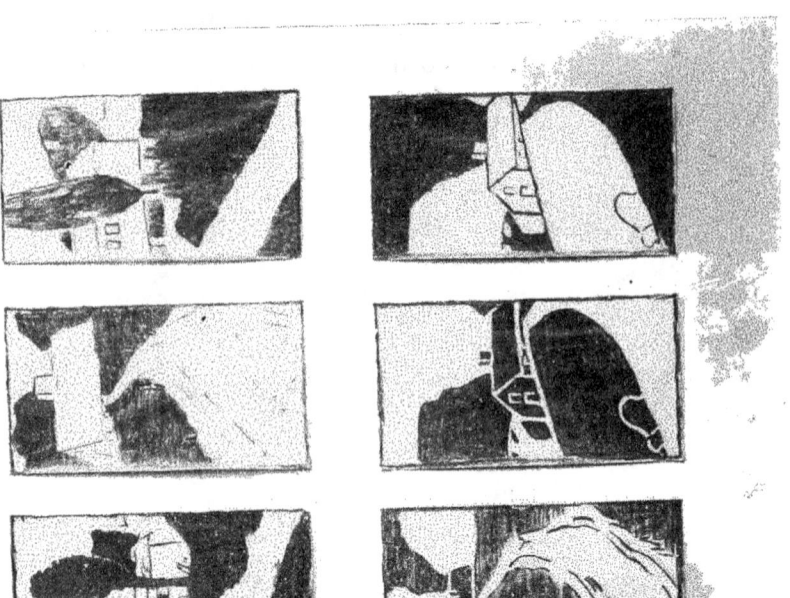

Grade VI. Landscapes. Arrangements in Black and White.

Grade VI. Poinsettia. Brush Drawing in Color. (Above.)
Grade III. Lilies. (Below.)

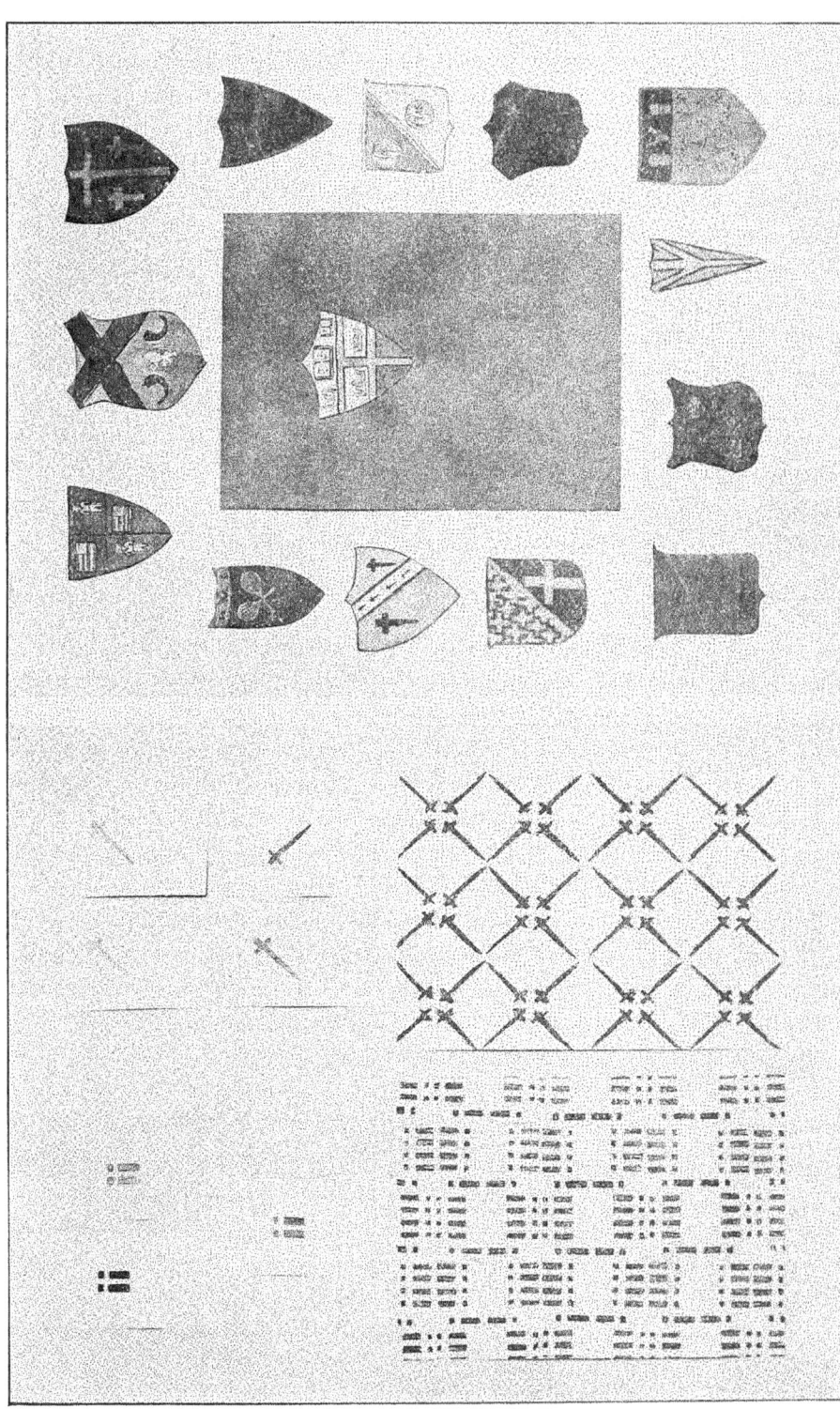

Grade VI. End Papers for Portfolios. Repetition in Grade VI. Coats-of-Arms for Portfolios. Original Ar-
Color. Stencils. rangements in Colors.

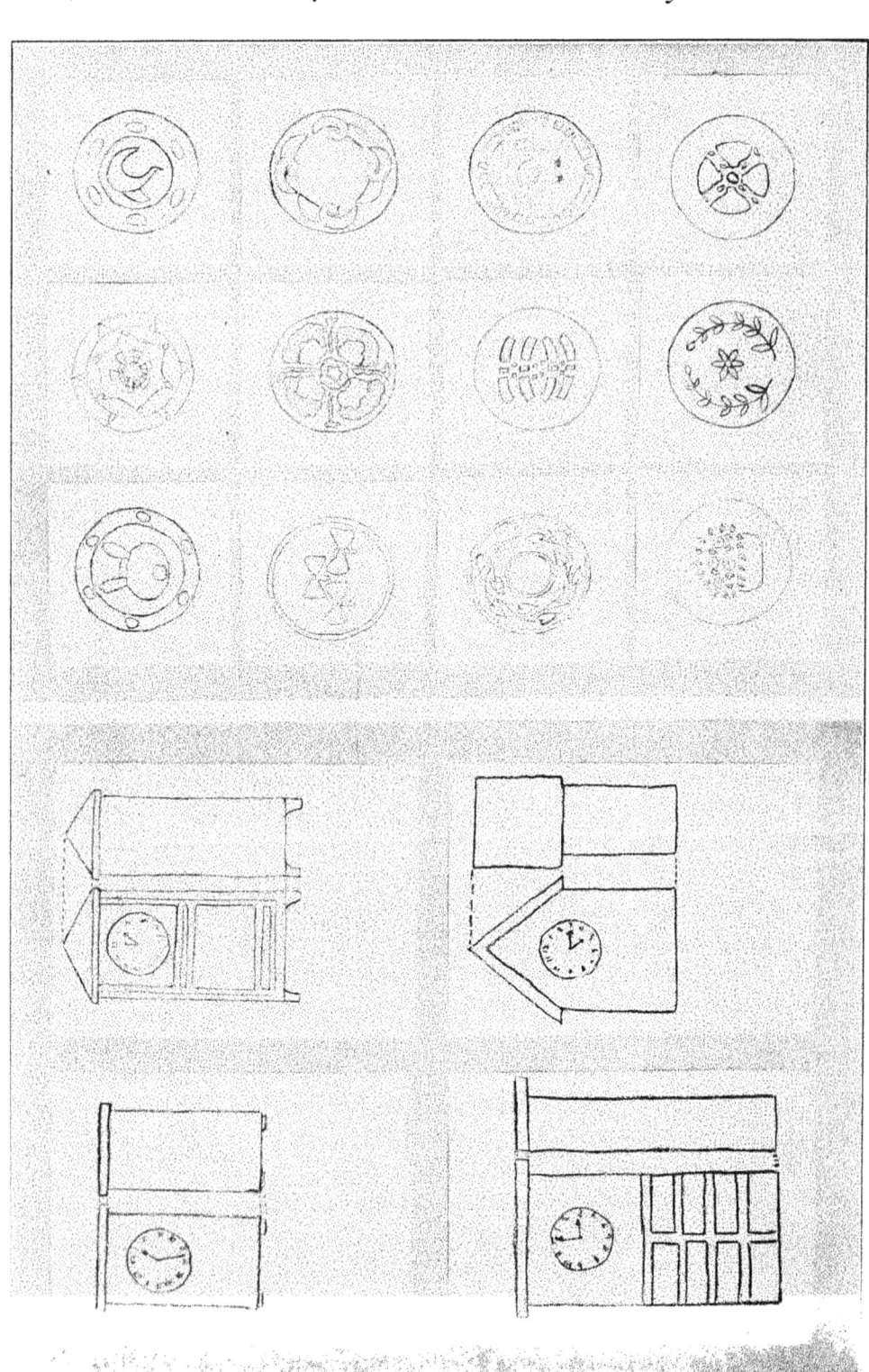

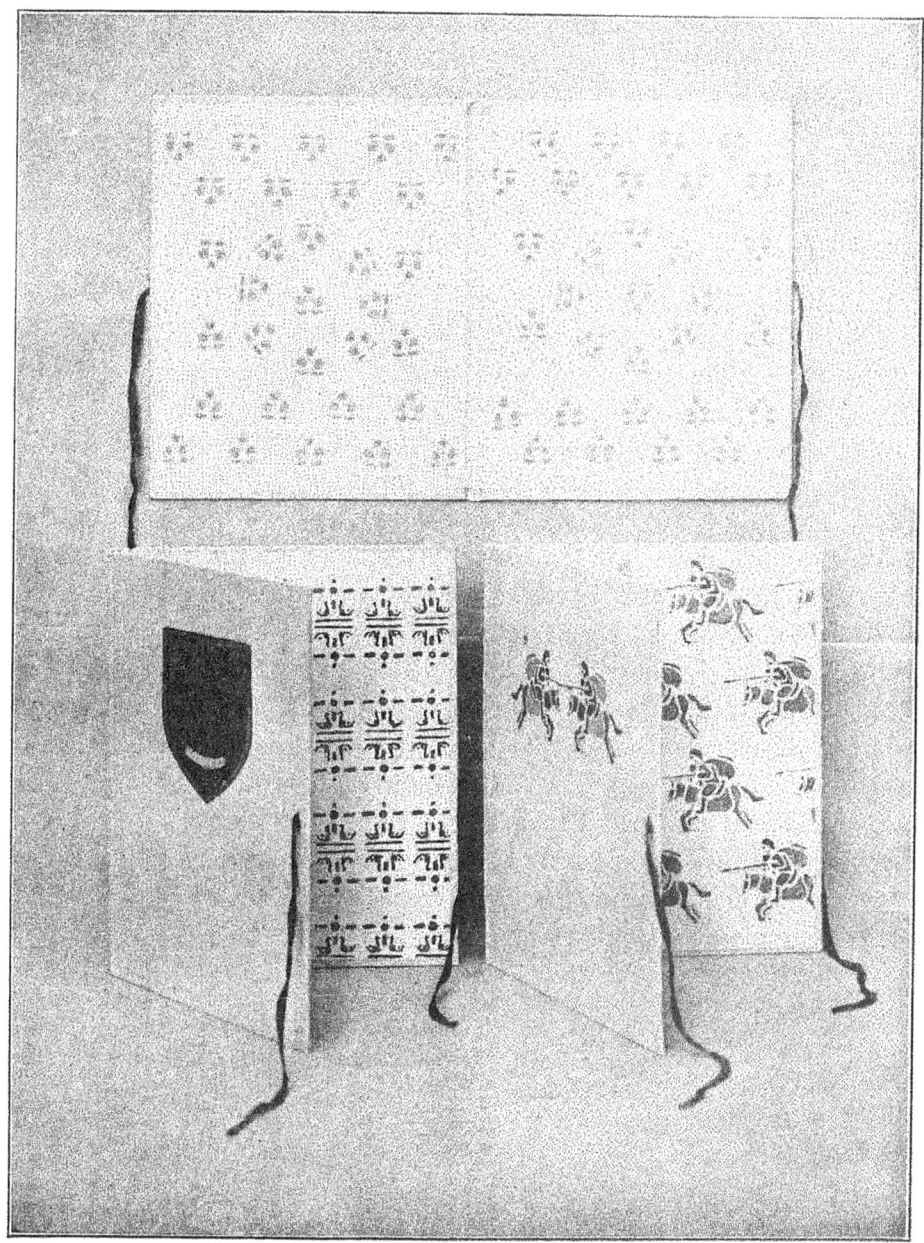

Grade VI   Portfolio.   Cutting and Pasting.

shown in houses in different positions, is found in the drawing and comparison of New York streets and those of mediaeval and country towns. These are carried into dark-and-light, and color. The perspective of the circle also comes in the study of certain flowers seen full front, three-quarters, and side view; in the poinsettia at Christmas time, and in the lily at Easter.

A substantial portfolio for school papers is a favorite problem in construction. The children make designs for their own stenciled end papers and, for the cover, a coat-of-arms of symbols whose meanings lie close to their own interests. Lettering is taken up in initials designed for the covers of their art portfolios, and the boys also use these on paper weights cast in their industrial art work. Lettering is also used in making posters. Figure drawing in sketches of schoolmates, colonial figures, and copies of good models, is done by this grade. Designs are made for clock cases, which are worked out in the industrial art class by the boys, who also frame one of their best sketches for the year; while the girls design patterns for a desk-pad and penwiper embroidered in their domestic art work.

The geographical study of Egypt is supplemented with the colored illustrations of that country by Jules Guerin, and a lecture on the art of Egypt is given by the head of the Fine Arts Department of Teachers College. Collections of good Coptic, Gothic, and modern designs are made and given to these children to study as illustrations of the ways in which others have successfully solved their own problems.

SUMMARY OF AN ILLUSTRATED CHRISTMAS LECTURE

The main thought that we aim to express is that it is not merely a peaceful subject which gives the restful feeling in art, but the harmonious relation of the lines, dark and light masses, and colors. Opposing lines produce restlessness, and when these lines are in extreme opposition they give a feeling of violence or war.

This idea is presented through the following pictures:

War: Illustrated in opposing lines.
  Metopes of the Parthenon—National Gallery, London.
  Carved Chest End of XVI Century—70 Cluny Museum.
  War—Winslow Homer.

Peace: Illustrated in repeating lines.
  Bearers of Wine Vessels—Parthenon Frieze.
  Sheep—Mauve, Metropolitan Museum.
  Presentation of the Virgin—Giotto, Santa Maria Novella, Florence.
  Morning—Corot, Louvre.

Nativities.
  Holy Night—Maratta, Dresden Gallery.
  Holy Night—Correggio, Dresden Gallery.
  Nativity—Francesca, National Gallery.
  Adoration of the Magi—Gozzoli, Riccardi Palace, Florence.
  Presentation in the Temple—Rembrandt, Mauritshuis, The Hague.

Madonnas.
  Sistine Madonna—Raphael, Dresden Gallery.
  Myer Madonna—Holbein, Dresden Gallery.
  Madonna and Child—Botticelli, Louvre.
  Madonna of the Rabbit—Titian, Louvre.
  Portrait of Lady with a Child—Romney, National Gallery.
  Elizabeth Van der Meersh and Her Four Daughters (detail from Baptism of Christ)—David, Museum, Bruges.

Angels.
  Angels (detail from Assumption)—Titian, Academy, Venice.
  Angels (detail from Frari Madonna)—Giovanni Bellini, Venice.

Lute Player (detail from Presentation in Temple)—Carpaccio, Academy, Venice.

Jolly People, like Santa Claus.
Nurse and Child—Hals, Frederichs Museum, Berlin.
Laughing Cavalier—Hals, Wallace Collection, London.
Miss Bowles—Reynolds, Wallace Collection, London.
Helena Van der Schalk—Ter Borch, Rijks Museum, Amsterdam.
"Good Papa Corot."
Bon Bock—Manet.

Peace in a Landscape.
Snow Scene—Hiroshige.

Peace in a Home.
Portrait of My Mother—Whistler, Luxembourg, Paris.

Peace With a Saint.
St. Genevieve Watching over the Sleeping City—Puvis de Chavannes, Panthéon, Paris.

Peace and Good Will in an Old Man's Face.
Walt Whitman—John Alexander, Metropolitan Museum.

PHYSICAL EDUCATION

The work in Physical Education is required of all pupils and is conducted by specially trained teachers in the various gymnasiums of the school. The time assignment is five twenty-minute periods per week for grades one and two, four twenty-minute periods for grades three and four, and three thirty-five-minute periods for grades five, six, and seven. The boys and girls are taught together in the first four grades, but in separate classes in the other grades. A thorough physical examination is given to each pupil by the school physician at least once a year. If this examination shows that the child's physical condition is such that he should not participate in the regular gymnastic work of his class, the teacher is notified and the parent is advised to provide special corrective treatment or exercises. Likewise, any facts that the class-room teacher or the gymnasium instructor should know are reported to her.

FIRST, SECOND, THIRD, AND FOURTH GRADES

The physical activity in the first four grades is furnished by games, dancing, apparatus work, freehand exercises, and marching. More than half the time is devoted to games and dancing, the game form being used in the apparatus work also. The object of the apparatus work is to develop control of the body with reference to external objects. However, this work is limited because it keeps so few children active at a time. Special emphasis is placed on rope climbing and practically all the children learn to climb before the end of the fourth year. About five minutes a day is devoted to freehand exercises which are accompanied by music. These exercises are chosen from activities within the child's experience, while in the third and fourth grades such exercises are chosen, so far as possible, as will increase proficiency in the games of skill, in dancing, and in apparatus work. All the exercises are used as a means to an

181

Job.......... for.......... _L_

Mend by......... Time...........

[Unusual mending time charged extra

Stab by........ No. Sect. _12_ ......Sew by

Before sewing, Score.... Press.... Strip S
[Scoring is necessary on stiff or heavy pa

Rate ....

end. Throughout all the work attention is given to the correction of faulty posture and to the physiological effect of the exercises. Marching is also used with special attention to carriage.

Balance exercises are used to a great extent. In a balance exercise the body naturally takes a correct position without consciousness of any particular part of the body. Constant use of such exercises has been found very helpful in gaining good carriage.

Through the grades, especially in the first and second years, the work is correlated with the music and reading work wherever possible. For instance, one year the First Grade dramatized "Cinderella," the "Pied Piper," and a little fairy tale of the "Elves and the Dwarfs" which they had been reading. In the song recital at the end of the year, the songs were accompanied by pantomime worked out in the gymnasium. The Second Grade interpreted nursery rhymes such as "The King of France," "Mistress Mary," and "Little-Bo-Peep."

FIFTH, SIXTH, AND SEVENTH GRADES: BOYS

The gymnasium work for the boys of the grammar grades consists of marching, calisthenics, and games. The corrective aspects of the calisthenics drills receive special attention. More than half the time is devoted to games, and this emphasis is justified not only by the splendid exercise afforded by the games, but by the opportunity they give for the development of honor, fairness, and team spirit. The boys of the Sixth and Seventh grades may spend one period each week in the swimming pool.

Two afternoons each week optional work of a recreative nature is open to the boys of these grades. In the fall and spring this time is spent on the athletic field in the seasonal games and sports, while during the winter months their attention is centered on basketball.

FIFTH, SIXTH, AND SEVENTH GRADES: GIRLS

The physical education of the girls of the grammar grades involves several forms of activity, such as freehand exercises, simple apparatus work, plays, games, and dancing.

Made in United States
Troutdale, OR
11/27/2025

42636850R00110